ESCAPE THE RAIN

FOR DRAGANA & FAMILY

[signature]

DEC 1, 2018
CALGARY . AB.
CANADA .

ESCAPE THE RAIN

Daryl Robbins

Library of Congress Control Number:		2015912136
ISBN:	Hardcover	978-1-5035-8996-4
	Softcover	978-1-5035-8995-7
	eBook	978-1-5035-8994-0

Print information available on the last page.

Rev. date: 09/18/2015

To order additional copies of this book, contact:
Xlibris
1-888-795-4274
www.Xlibris.com
Orders@Xlibris.com
719048

CONTENTS

WORLD HISTORY
1979

Oil spills pollute ocean waters of the Atlantic and the Gulf of Mexico (January 1, June 8, and July 21). Ohio agrees to pay $675,000 to families of those who died and were injured in the Kent State University shootings (January 4). Vietnam and Vietnam-backed Cambodian insurgents announce the fall of Phnom Penh, the capital of Cambodia, and the collapse of the Pol Pot regime (January 7). Shah leaves Iran after the year of turmoil (January 16); revolutionary forces under Muslim leader Ayatollah Ruhollah Khomeini take over (February 1 et seq.). The nuclear power plant accident at Three Mile Island, Pennsylvania, releases radiation (March 28). Conservatives win British election; Margaret Thatcher becomes the new prime minister (May 3). Carter and Brezhnev sign the SALT II agreement (June 14). Nicaragua president Gen. Anastasio Somoza Debayle resigns and flees to Miami (July 17); Sandinistas form the government (July 19). Earl Mountbatten of Burma, 79, British World War II hero, and three others are killed by blast on fishing boat off Irish coast (August 27); two IRA members are accused (August 30). Iranian militants seize the U.S. Embassy in Teheran and hold hostages (November 4). Soviet invasion of Afghanistan stirs world protests (December 27).

Crowds in Timisoara

Nicolae Ceausescu

The Reign Begins... Nicolae Ceausescu, the son of a peasant, was born in 1918. Early on, he became active in the Romanian Communist movement and was later arrested as a revolutionary; he spent the late 1930s and early '40s in prison, where he became acquainted with the future first secretary of the Romanian Communist party, Gheorghe Gheorghiu-Dej. After escaping in 1944, Ceausescu held a variety of posts within Communist party and government ranks after the Communist takeover in 1948. He soon became a member of the party's central committee and then, in 1955, a member of the politburo. Upon Gheorghiu-Dej's death in March 1965, he was chosen first secretary of the central committee of the Communist party; and in December 1967, he assumed the office of the president of the state council. As supreme leader, he continued his mentor's policy of nationalism and independence from the USSR within the context of Marxism-Leninism. He promoted closer relations with the People's Republic of China and with the West, as well as industrial and agricultural development. His domestic rule, however, was marked by frequently disastrous economic schemes and became increasingly repressive and corrupt. In December 1989, an uprising in the city of Timişoara, and the subsequent deaths of protestors, led to a demonstration in Bucharest, the capital of Romania, which, joined by the army, led to the arrest and execution of him and his wife, Elena.

http://www.ceausescu.org/

PROLOGUE

Wherever you are, whether on the street, at work, in a store, or traveling or camping, we have all met many different people. You may have detected an accent and wondered, or maybe even asked them, where they were originally from. Of course, if you are like me, you must have pondered why they left their homes and chose Canada as their newly adopted country. Some may have left behind a career or even their family. Most had to learn a new language, had to try to fit in, just to start all over again. Every immigrant has a story to tell. This is ours, told through the experience of my wife, Ofelia Rain, and me, Doru Rain. We dedicate it to all the other Romanians who left during the reign of Ceausescu.

Doru and Ofelia Rain

FROM THE AUTHOR

In some small way, I hope to have been able to preserve the memories of such a magnificent journey for family, and for friends, to keep history alive. For me, the hours spent questioning and dictating were a journey in itself. I felt firsthand from afar, in the comfort of my home, the dangers and the anxiety and traveled the road less taken. I hope my kids will read and experience the journey I took through the eyes of their faux grandparents—Doru and Ofelia Rain.

R.C. Robbins

Princeton '90

00hrs00mins: Rain Is on the Way

Jesuus Christ, it is cold! I was shivering. I crossed my arms, held my elbows in my hands, and squeezed my chest. I could feel the warmth coming back into my core. I stared up at the ceiling from my bed. I thought to myself, *Don't April showers bring May flowers?* Not this year. Not in Calgary. Snow was still piled high. My window was half frosted. The thermometer attached to the wall outside read -20°C. It was cold.

Tonight I battled with an overactive mind. I lost my pillowcase in my turning. I remembered the numbers on my clock glared red: 2:22 a.m., 3:33 a.m., and 4:44 a.m. And then, as if no time had passed, the clock buzzer blared out. It was already 8:00 a.m. It startled me from my shallow sleep. Between the interruptions, I dreamt of my wife, Ofelia, and my son, Liviu. I could feel the smoothness of Ofelia's plum brandy brunette hair that hung down just below her shoulders. I could feel the smoothness of her bronze colored cheeks as if I held them now. And I could see her full smile, with a small gap in her two front teeth. It made me happy. I thought to myself, *Were they OK? Where were they now?* It had been more than two years and thousands of kilometers since I had last seen them. Their faces were as vivid now as they were then.

The gray, overcast morning turned from a light snow to a bright fresh blue sky. It was going to be a great day. Instead of lying here thinking any longer, I decided to get on the road a little early and enjoy the morning. By the time I got out the door, only a few cloud pillows hung over the windless sky. I heard an airplane out the car window. Maybe I was just day dreaming as I glanced skyward, squinting at several white jet trails.

I noticed my rear view mirror was slightly askew. As I lifted my right hand to make the adjustment, the red blotches in the whites of my brown eyes glared back at me. I hadn't been drinking. Jesus, my thin brown hair was out of control too. I could see strands of gray. So I pushed it to the side, the way I had always worn it. It must have grown just like my handlebar mustache. I worried about how else I might have changed. Arching my back, I strained my neck to see my chest and belly. My 165-pound frame hadn't gained any weight. It wasn't muscular, nor frail, just normal; in height too, not imposing as some guys. *Who wanted to be imposing anyway*, I quipped to myself. *Better to be bighearted*, I thought, nodding as though I sought my own approval. Maybe my hairline had receded a little; there was definitely more skin on my prominent brow. But I felt happy anyway. My big smile attested to that. I really am fortunate.

Still, my heart throbbed, and my stomach rumbled with anticipation. I felt like a spring ready to release all its stress as the moment of truth came ever so near.

August 18, 1979, 9:00 a.m.: Knock! Knock! *That must be Ludwig at the door*, I thought, staring out the window across the other block building. Our neighbor was busily working in her kitchen. Was she cooking? She glanced over at me, and I made no effort to avert my eyes even though I realized I had been spying on her, watching her every move. I cared not for what she was doing. *Knock! Knock! Knock!* Oh, Ludwig, I returned from my daydream. "Can you get it, baby?" I implored Ofelia as I tried to concentrate on finishing the remainder of the *slanina cu boia* (pig fat with paprika) on my plate. Ludwig Rorig was at our apartment door, ready for our trip to Bazias.

"*Buna dimineata* (good morning), Ofelia . . . Doru . . . Liviu," he exclaimed, nodding and pausing as he looked at each of us in turn. His eyes wandered throughout the room. Our stuff was everywhere. But he admired our handiwork anyway. We had just installed a hardwood floor, which he helped finish yesterday. Ludwig unbuttoned his jacket, apparently to free his arms, as he kneeled down for a reinspection. With his hand, he swept a large area to feel its texture. It still smelled of lacquer with a touch of oak. His eyes sparkled with satisfaction. He slowly stood up, turned, and made his way to our single table, where he sat down across from me, next to Liviu. "I hear you are going to have a birthday next week. How old are you going to be?" he asked Liviu.

"*Cinci* (five)." Liviu barely responded as he ate his cereal.

"Are you ready to go Doru?" Ludwig asked.

Resita : Doru, Liviu and Ofelia Rain

He should have guessed from the bread and *slanina* (bacon fat) that remained on my plate. However, unlike his normal self, Ludwig was unable to hide his excitement for our journey. "Just a second, Ludwig," I said. I took a final sip of my coffee and an oversized bite of my bread, went to the closet, put on a light jacket, and slipped on my shoes. I sat back onto the chair, my mouth still half full, and reached down to finish tying my laces. Ofelia placed a leather satchel on the table for us.

"You can use this bag to carry the fish from Bazias," she insisted.

As I stood up, straightening my clothes, Ofelia leaned against me as I started toward the door. She took hold of my hand and gave me a kiss on the lips. Liviu got down from the table too and ran over to us. I kneeled, and he gave me a great big firm bear hug. That felt so good, both of them so close to me.

"Be a good boy for your mommy now. OK?" I pleaded with him. Ludwig too got up and met us in front of the door.

"Don't forget to say hi to your grandparents for Liviu and me," Ofelia reminded me.

"Of course, I will, baby. *Te iubesc* (I love you)." I gave her one last kiss at the door before my voice had a chance to crack and forced back any tears. "*Pa* (bye)."

Barely two steps outside the apartment, I turned back only to see Ofelia looking at me. She came close again, and I took her left cheek in the palm of my right hand and pulled her close. I kissed her eyebrow and again her forehead. Second thoughts ran about inside my head. I hoped she couldn't tell.

That's how Ludwig Rorig, my workmate, and I began our journey from Reşiţa, Romania. We were off to my grandparents' home in the small village of Bazias on the north eastern shore of the Danube River. I grew up there as a kid. It would be easier to buy some fresh fish for our celebration of the liberation of Romania from Germany during WWII, August 23, 1944. Besides, the celebrations of St. Preobrazenie gave us a perfect excuse to enjoy the festivities in Bazias this weekend. Villagers from surrounding hamlets would congregate there the evening prior. There was always a party before the service at the Savvas Monastery on Sunday morning. Ofelia and Liviu had to stay in Reşiţa. Liviu was going to school this morning, and Ofelia had to work at the blood bank this weekend.

The concrete stairway, as in every apartment block, was unevenly poured and poorly lit. The single original light bulb had been stolen some time ago. No one ever replaced it. What kind of bullshit place do we live in? We concentrated on our footing as we descended. I remembered we needed a couple extra plastic bags . . . for the fish. We could stop at the department store. The store was five hundred meters down the road on the way to the bus station. I always hated going through our small parking lot. The trash bin, as always, was overflowing. The rotten food created an abhorrent stench. Unfortunately, it was the only place where kids from the block could play.

Traffic on the main road was minimal this morning. There was only the typical honking of a few cars. Several vehicles, however, Lauries, AROs, and Dacias, were already parked irregularly in front of the department store. Mainly dark-skinned gypsies mulled about the vehicles. They had on their typically colorful yet dirty clothing. The women wore purple and yellow and gold head scarves. They were selling whatever goods they had from their opened trunks. I saw a few scrawny dead chickens, potatoes in burlap bags, and corn with the husk still on. We didn't need anything from them today.

Once we got past the blockade, we pulled at several of the entrance doors. Only a single door was unlocked. Crowd control of sorts, I suspected. Inside it was dank, like a cold sweat, and somewhat dark. My eyes took a few moments to adjust to the poor lighting. After walking around and looking a little, we weren't any closer to finding the plastic bags we sought. As had become usual, the display cases were empty. We hoped that the sales lady behind one of the counters could direct us to the right location. She stood there talking to another colleague. She pretended to work and paid us little attention. Typical as one would say: "They pretend to pay us and we pretend to work." We moved into her direct view before we finally got her attention. They had none there. In fact, they had nothing there at all. She sent us to the library across the square. She thought we could find some good ones for sale. Why in the hell plastic bags would be sold at the library rather than the department store was beyond me. That's just how far Romania had sunken.

Back in early 1979, I distinctly remember when Ceausescu gave his daily speech on the single TV channel. Usually, Ofelia and I paid little to no attention to his daily communist rhetoric. But for some reason, that day was different. As always, he stood behind a podium. That stupid fedora was on his head. Ceausescu spoke of how the national debt had grown to substantial size. It was now time to rectify the situation. Each and every Romanian had their small part to share in this. And it was now that time for all of us to pull up our trousers and tighten our belts to make Romania stronger for the future.

Horrifyingly enough, we pulled our belts sooner and yanked them more taut than we could ever have imagined. Not months nor weeks passed but only days after this ominous broadcast when the store shelves became bare. Even food became scarce. As the weeks passed, there was really nothing to buy. Nothing of nutritional value was left. The government began issuing ration cards. We were only allowed a little cheese, a loaf of bread, and a few grams of meat per week. They came at irregular times. Milk was basically nonexistent except for children under the age of two. Their allotment was insufficient.

We found ourselves standing in ever-growing lines to get our share. Oftentimes we would stop in one on our way home from work. Generally, we didn't know what was being distributed; but nonetheless, we wanted our share. Our pockets always had money, just in case. There was always someone in the queue who told political jokes. Everyone worried they would be accused. But it didn't stop us. Frequently, the lines were so long that we had to ask those ahead and behind to hold our positions as we sought a nearby place to urinate. What's even worse, the store would close at nine o'clock, and we would be left with nothing.

On several occasions, I remember standing in a line only to see the person purportedly distributing the food come out and wave us away. Evidently, they had nothing left to sell. Unfortunately, the line lengthened rather than dispersed. It wasn't until the lights were dimmed and the doors were locked that it was obvious there really was nothing left. We went home dejected. Other than the money in our pockets, there was nothing to show for our patience.

We passed the *alimentar* (corner store). I noticed the shelves were bare. Two skinny rats foraged in the window, as if pleading to find a scrap of food.

In the square one afternoon, a truck from the cooperatives in the country stopped to sell bags of potatoes. People swarmed the vehicle from all directions. It was like a pack of monkeys climbing from all directions to get inside and get their bag. I jumped into the fray as well, landing nearly on top of a frail-looking lady. I grabbed. She grabbed. There was only one bag left near us. I wanted it badly; I tugged and she screamed at me.

"I have nothing to feed my children!"

Surprised by her ferocity, the prize slipped from my hand. Shock hit me hard by how we had become. So I helped her unload the bag to the road below.

The library actually had lots of crunched-up bags for sale, probably from earlier deliveries of new communist propaganda books. They were always in full supply. There were bags of all sizes but mostly clear and pretty thick. After rummaging awhile, and inspecting them as best we could, we chose a couple of clear ones about the size of a big garbage bag. On our way to the cashier, we checked them further for small holes and tears. I really wanted to blow some air into them to test their worthiness but dared not in fear of raising some sort of suspicion among the onlookers. When our turn came, we paid a couple lei for the two bags and folded them into the satchel before continuing on our journey to the bus station.

Now the streets were busy with people walking here and there. Closer to the station, more people carried large linen bags between two people. The dual bus and train station had become the focal point for most transport since Ceausescu took presidency. Now very few people could afford to pay for gas. Most times the supply was empty. Once Ceausescu took control of the party and became the eternal president, the communists confiscated all vehicles.

Near the bus station payment window, I recognized a man from Socol—Pera. He had been visiting his son, an engineer, in Reşiţa. My father had known Pera well, and his son and I were schoolmates in Socol. I introduced Ludwig to him. We chatted about our families for some half an hour as we waited for our bus. When it finally arrived, late as per usual, out from the bus stepped farmers from the countryside. Some had come with bags full of semirotten vegetables from the commune. They came to sell and trade in the city. Most were empty-handed looking for something, anything. There was nothing available in the countryside. Things there had gotten much worse since Ceausescu's TV announcement.

Eventually, Ludwig and I were able to find two seats together. Pera picked an empty seat a little further ahead. It took quite some time for the passengers to load the bus with their myriad of items. Even older couples, some helped by their friends or relatives, brought large, heavy sacks on board. They struggled to maneuver their large sacks down the aisle. They jammed them as best they could onto the floor between their seat and the one ahead. When we all finally settled down, either a person or someone's belongings occupied every seat. The engine clambered, and the gears ground. A great plume of black partially burnt smoke rose. And the bus lurched as the driver hit the gas. It was only 11:00 a.m., and already, the bus was getting warm from all the activity. I took my jacket off, made myself comfortable, and began to stare out the window at the cement block buildings of systematization that made up Reşiţa and every other city in Romania.

My anxiety, and the rocking and rolling of the vehicle, must have shook me into a daydream, pondering my future, reflecting on my past. Our lives were about to change.

Tatti: A Flood of Emotion

September on the Black Sea is wonderful. The beach, the women, the parties: good times. It wasn't all fun though as I had gone there to take an officer's exam for the navy. On my return to work, I decided to visit my family in the village of Bazias where I had grown up. I spent a nice yet brief time there. As usual, Mom and Dad were fine. They were busy preparing for the harvest season. My younger brother, Nicolae, remained distant; and my youngest brother, Viorel, was his usual mischievous self. They implored me to stay and help with the crops. They knew though that I had to return to my work in Timișoara. Everything was normal.

Back in Timișoara, the grind of work continued. By chance, I decided to venture to the post office to inquire about the mail. It had been only a couple of weeks since I had last talked to my family, so I really wasn't expecting anything from them. There weren't any letters. But there was a phone there, so I decided to call them.

Resita : Doru at Work

Just a few years earlier, my father had joined the communist party in order to take a job monitoring the water level of the Danube. We needed the phone to call a centralized point three times daily, so the government installed it for us. The operator did her thing, and sure enough, I was finally connected to her.

Mom was quite distraught. She informed me that Dad had taken ill only a week after my short visit. He had complained of a headache shortly after having arrived at our cornfield. That morning at the crack of dawn, with Viorel sitting on the bicycle handles, Mom straddling the crossbar, and Dad sitting on the seat, he peddled their way to our government-allotted field. It was some five kilometers up the road toward the larger village of Socol. There, the hills flattened into fields where we could grow our illicit vegetables between the rows of government-approved corn.

As morning passed, Dad had complained of a headache. He was a tough man who rarely complained of any discomfort. So

Mom told him to get himself and Viorel home to his mother in Bazias. They both concurred. Maybe he could get a ride to the general hospital in Moldova Nouă some twenty-five kilometers southeast. Later that evening, upon her return from the fields, she learned that he had indeed gotten a ride. So with some trepidation, borne from the fact that he had never complained of any ailment before, she decided to go see him the next day after she finished harvesting the field.

The hospital in Moldova Nouă was poorly equipped to deal with anything more than the common cold. The staff monitored him for a few days. They gave him no idea of his ailment. Mom could find no explanations. Either the doctors really didn't know or they were just being unapproachable as was the common practice back then. However, they informed her that should his condition remain unchanged, more tests would be required. He would need to go to one of the larger hospitals at Oravița, Reşiţa, or Timişoara. They reassured her that they would inform her of any transfer.

At that point, Mom said she decided to go home. She couldn't afford to stay there. The hospital was unable to administer any information anyway. Besides, she was one of the fortunate few who had a housephone. She could stay there and await news.

She had received a call informing her that he had been admitted to the hospital in Oravița. And just now, she had just heard he was going to be transferred again but didn't know where.

As we talked on the phone, she became even more distraught. I decided to make arrangements to locate and visit him.

There were three possible cities to begin searching: Oravița, Resiţa, or Timişoara. I thought it best to start in Oravița. Someone there could tell me for sure where he was being transferred. Besides, I surmised that he likely wouldn't have been sent to Timişoara unless he was really very ill. From his demeanour a month ago, that seemed farfetched as well. Conveniently, there was a direct train from Timişoara to Oravița.

Five hours later, the train screeched to a halt at the Oravița station. The remaining walk allowed me to stretch my muscles. I stopped at the hospital registration desk to find information on my father, Nicolae. The registrar found his name. She noted that he had been discharged. *Hmm, Dad must have gone home,* I thought. With little more information, I decided to return to Timișoara. Fortunately, the same train was leaving in just an hour's time, so back home I went.

Timișoara, October 4, 1970, 6:30 a.m.: It was just the beginning of another work day. I walked mindlessly, head bowed, pushed along by the mass of workers. Near the factory gates, I was shocked to see my mother, Viorica. She threw herself at me. She was heaving and crying. Tears flowed down her cheeks. I caught her with my outstretched arms.

"*Ce faci?* (What's wrong?)," I asked, propping her up. "What are you doing here?"

"Your father is in the hospital. He is very sick. The doctors won't tell me from what," she rambled on, sobbing. "And I don't know to which hospital he has been admitted."

"Jesuus Christ!" I murmured.

Somehow I calmed Mom's weeping and wailing. I explained that I would be back shortly. I left her at the factory gates while I went into the factory to discuss the situation with my supervisor. Sympathetic to my situation, he asked if he could help. I wasn't quite sure how he could help. It was clear that, first, I must find my father and take things from there.

On my return, Mom broke into tears again. Her bonnet was askew and her round skirt in disarray. Together, we gathered ourselves and made a plan before heading to the bus station. There are several large hospitals in Timișoara, each with its own specialization. One specialized in ears, mouth, and throat; one in burns; and another in lungs. Our search began with what little Mom remembered from Dad in the cornfield. All she knew was that Dad had a headache.

At the first hospital, we went directly to the registrar, as in Oraviţa, to see if Nicolae Rain had been admitted. He had not. After some discussion with the gentleman, we headed off to another with no luck as well. The registrar at the third hospital found his name but wouldn't allow us to enter the building. Pleading our case, not knowing Dad's condition, the registrar was firm in his resolve to follow the letter of the restriction of visitors outside the appropriate timings.

Dejected, we took his room number and waited for the second visiting hours to begin. Sitting on a wooden bench, we wondered what could have befallen him in such a short period. Dad looked great only a month before. And at forty-two, his tough demeanour hadn't lost any of its spark. What kind of virus could he have caught so quickly?

At the awaited time, Mom and I ascended the stairs to the second story and started down the hallway, in what we decided was the correct direction. The hospital smelled of urine mixed with antiseptic. It was as though disinfectants were losing the battle. There were so many people in each of the rooms on both sides of the hall. Dad's room was no exception, with twenty to thirty people lying in beds separated by a mere foot on either side.

Dad was near the middle. He looked twenty kilograms lighter. His face was pallid and drawn. A bandage, stained with blood, was wrapped around his head. The heat and humidity combined with what little air circulation there was only intensified the smell of antiseptics. As we approached, he appeared to be conscious and said hello to mother. Me though, he did not recognize. He remembered somewhat when I told him who I was, but he seemed puzzled, unable to put my face with the name. That bandage concealed something much more worrisome than a virus I surmised it must be.

Shocked, in disbelief, I sought out a nurse for information. She told me nothing. So with no information forthcoming, I demanded to see a doctor. I even went searching for one. As in

Oraviţa, either no one knew or no one wanted to tell anything. To add to our dismay, as patiently and as long as we had waited to see Dad, they urgently rushed us out of the room as visiting hours had ended.

We had finally seen him. The bandage made it clear that he was seriously ill. And it was obvious that he had had an operation of sorts along his journey to Timişoara. We were told nothing. Baffled, we cried and cried.

The next morning, Mom had to leave for home to continue with the Danube monitoring. She could not afford to jeopardize her income at this time. I too returned to the factory. I had to get permission for a couple of days' leave in order to tend to Dad. Then it was back to the hospital to see Dad. I wanted to learn as much as I could. This time, Dad's doctor was there and, as usual, gave me little insight into his condition. Jesus. It was as if he were keeping it a secret from me. Maybe he thought we were not educated enough to understand. Maybe he was too conceited. Who knows! After persistent prying though, he reluctantly informed me. Dad would be operated on sometime the following day.

What to do now? I still didn't know what ailed him. What's even worse, I still had no idea how sick he was or even about the nature of the operation. I stayed with Dad for a good part of the day. I returned in the late afternoon with some fruits from the market. He was poorly fed at the hospital. I thought he would like some grapes and pears. They were his favorites. Maybe it would lift his spirits a little. Moments after eating, he vomited onto his bedsheets. I folded them up and tossed it into a heap on the floor.

"Visiting hours is now over! Please proceed to the nearest exit," squawked an impersonal female voice from the overhead speakers.

There laid Dad, semicomatose, all alone in that room crammed with thirty others.

Awake at six the next morning, work seemed to be the only thing to do. Dad would have his operation sometime today. Who knew when? I'll go see him directly after work, I conjectured. I remembered too that I had a date with a girl, Viorica, whom I had met some short time before. So work it was until five in the afternoon.

Viorica met me on the park bench nearest my apartment. My mind just wasn't with her. Dad must have had his operation by now. She came along on the visit. The light-rail ride, as it swayed, sometimes abruptly, from side to side down the street to the hospital, was a welcome distraction from having to discuss Dad's condition.

Focused with a single purpose, we passed by the registrar and climbed the stairs to the second floor. We turned to the right. I could see through his room door. Something was different. I had to glance back at the number on the door. I questioned whether I had misread it. It was the right room. Dad's bed now lay vacant. New sheets were piled on top. "Where is he?" I blurted out loud.

I checked out the other beds in the room. Dad still wasn't there. An elder gentleman recognized me and smiled.

"Your dad's not here," he softly spoke.

"Where is he then?" I asked him.

"They moved him to another hospital today for his operation. I am not sure which one," he replied.

Thanking him, gently shaking his hand, and muttering to myself, I wondered why someone didn't tell me. Where could they have taken him? I assumed he was at the hospital across the road.

We clambered down the stairs past the registrar. I flung open the doors, and we ran across the street. This time, with no idea of his whereabouts, we stopped at the registrar. Gasping for breath, I asked an official if they had admitted Nicolae Rain. Carefully, he fingered the list in his book.

"What is your name?" he asked. I answered.

"What are you doing here in Timişoara?" he asked. I gave him a brief explanation.

"And who is your friend?" he interrogated me. My patience was running short.

"*Please*, sir, I don't have time for this. Please just tell me where I can find him," I pleaded.

A silence gripped his face, which brought a tingle to my spine. A foreboding sense of uncertainty played upon me. "I am afraid your father has passed away," he said in a forlorn tone.

Sweat dampened my undershirt. How could a nineteen-year-old boy, who thought he was a man, be expected to handle such news?

"He has been taken to the morgue," he said matter-of-factly. "You cannot see him this evening."

"Jesuus Christ! What do I do now?" I shuddered.

The registrar then sat me down and explained what I needed to do. I needed to buy a casket. I needed to get a vehicle from work. Then and only then could I come back and get Dad. It was going to be a long drive to Bazias. But first, I needed to inform Mom. I just didn't know how.

I telephoned Mom right away. She was heart stricken. She cried and cried. I was in shock. I couldn't think straight. Before she hung up, she said she would take the train and be right on her way.

Where would I get the truck and where would I buy a casket? Never mind the most pressing problem—money. Where could I get enough to pay for everything? Fortunately, Viorica was thinking straight. She stayed with me to help with the dilemma Dad had left us. My neighbor was kind enough to lend me some money. I hoped to get the rest as an advance from work.

My supervisor arranged for me to meet the factory manager the next day. In the morning, I went down to the train station and waited for Mom to arrive. Contemplating Dad's life made it even worse. Life is so fragile. He was born the first child of ten in 1926.

Rain Nicolae	Dad	Lived in Bazias. He was born out of wedlock and given his mother's maiden name.
Iacubov Rujita	Sister	At age sixteen, she fell from a mulberry tree next to the Danube. She broke her back and never walked again. At age twenty-one, she had a child out of wedlock. The father was never revealed. She lived her life in Bazias. Her surname is a mystery.
Iojici Mirko	Brother	Died of an apparent suicide by hanging after an argument with Rujita. The argument may have had something to do with him putting "hot" sauce on her child's lips in an attempt to stop him from being breast-fed.
Iojici Angela	Sister	Moved to Ploiesti.
Iojici Milita	Sister	Went to jail for approximately one year after the police found her newborn son buried in the cornfield. The child survived. Her husband was sentenced for six years.
Iojici Sretko	Brother	Lived in Bazias.
Iojici Zoran	Brother	Lived in Bazias.
Iojici Florian	Brother	Lived in Carancebes
Iojici	Sister	Died at birth.
Iojici Sofia	Sister	Lives near Timişoara.

Life is too tough. He was just a bit shorter than me and fought for what he had. Life is so difficult. He helped Grandpa raise the family by working on the farm. Life is too short.

He was only forty-two. I was only nineteen.

Mom and I bought a simple wooden casket. It was a strong casket, handmade. No ornaments though. My supervisor arranged everything else. We got a truck, some extra money, and even a full tank of gas.

We decided to buy Dad some clothes on the way to the morgue. I figured someone there would dress him. I assumed too much again; the task was left to Mom. I just couldn't bring myself to help. He looked fine in them. I placed him in the casket. I can't recall a bandage on his head.

Before we left, the coroner handed me the death certificate.

Cause of death: Encephalitis

Finally, we knew how he died and why his head was bandaged. That was all we ever could find out.

At twelve, we started our journey to Bazias. Dad was in the casket in the back. It was another hot day. The road was bumpy as always. It took us seven hours and several gas stops. I looked at the cemetery before we got to Bazias. Fresh dirt was piled in our plot. Thankfully, someone had already dug his grave.

As we pulled onto the main dirt road, the villagers were waiting. They joined in behind as we proceeded to the front of his home. Everyone from Bazias was there, all sixty of them, including Grandma Liubita, Grandpa Jivko, and my younger brothers, Nicolae and Viorel. All wore black.

At the house, most stood behind the truck. The sorrow showed on their faces. Tears dripped from their eyes. It was all too surreal as several of the men dragged Dad's casket from the truck. They brought him into our home's main room, placing him on the table. It was a clear day. It was hot for October, maybe in the thirties.

Bazias : Dad's Death - Doru holding Viorel, Viorica and Nicolae

Inside the small house, Grandma had covered each mirror with a cloth. Wailing and weeping, everyone took a turn in the room. The priest swung his silver *cadelnita* to and fro. Smoke, the eerie smell of incense, prayers, and crying filled the house. What light there was inside was dim. The sun was setting over the Danube. My heart was heavy. I could sense their sorrow. Somehow I had become a spectator as I watched from the corner of the room. Each mourner kneeled in front of Dad in the casket.

"Why has this happened to you? Why couldn't it be me? How did this happen?" Crying, chanting, praying.

"How could you get so sick so fast? Why did this happen to you?" Crying, chanting, praying.

At the end of the ordeal, we all went wearily to sleep. Dad lay in his casket in front of us.

The singing of a rooster broke the silence of the night. It signaled the beginning of a new day. We all began to move. Mom and Grandma fussed over Dad. They fixed his cap and the white cloth that covered him. Directly thereafter, as if preplanned, the priest gently tapped at the door. Most of the previous night's mourners followed him too. Again, as per script, the priest lit the *cadelnita*. He swung it to and fro. With its smoke and scent, and the background praying of the priest, the scene was set. A group among the family and his closest friends, maybe eight in all, formed alongside *Tata* in his casket. We were each given a large white candle. We lit them before the priest could continue. Once organized, in what seemed to be predetermined places, we raised *Tata*. We carried him on our shoulders. He left his home for the last time. The monastery wasn't far. It was just down the dirt road. The monastery was already filled with the townsfolk. The priest prayed in Serbian for the soul of Rain Nicolae.

Bazias : Savas Monestery

At the end of the service, those same pallbearers lifted the casket onto their shoulders. We carried it up the main road to the cemetery. After walking for fifty meters, the priest chanted and prayed. We laid the casket at our feet. The smoke and the aroma wafted gently above in the still morning.

A boat horn signaled in the distance.

¹The LORD is my shepherd; I shall not want. ²He maketh me to lie down in green pastures: he leadeth me beside the still waters. ³He restoreth my soul: he leadeth me in the paths of righteousness for his name's sake. ⁴Yea, though I walk through the valley of the shadow of death, I will fear no evil: for thou art with me; thy rod and thy staff they comfort me. ⁵Thou preparest a table before me in the presence of mine enemies: thou anointest my head with oil; my cup runneth over. ⁶Surely goodness and mercy shall follow me all the days of my life: and I will dwell in the house of the LORD forever.

We lifted the casket up again on to our shoulders. We marched slowly onward for another one hundred meters. Again, we placed the casket at our feet. The priest chanted and prayed some more in Serbian.

¹When he was come down from the mountain, great multitudes followed him. ²And, behold, there came a leper and worshipped him, saying, Lord, if thou wilt, thou canst make me clean. ³And Jesus put forth his hand, and touched him, saying, I will; be thou clean. And immediately his leprosy was cleansed. ⁴And Jesus saith unto him, See thou tell no man; but go thy way, shew thyself to the priest, and offer the gift that Moses commanded, for a testimony unto them. ⁵And when Jesus was entered into Capernaum, there came unto him a centurion, beseeching him, ⁶and saying, Lord, my servant lieth at home sick of the palsy, grievously tormented. ⁷And Jesus saith unto him, I will come and heal him. ⁸The centurion answered and said, Lord, I am not worthy that thou shouldest come under my roof: but speak the word only, and my servant shall be healed. ⁹For I am a man under authority, having soldiers under me: and I say to this man, Go, and he goeth; and to another,

Come, and he cometh; and to my servant, Do this, and
he doeth it. [10]When Jesus heard it, he marvelled, and said
to them that followed, Verily I say unto you, I have not
found so great faith, no, not in Israel. [11]And I say unto
you, That many shall come from the east and west, and
shall sit down with Abraham, and Isaac, and Jacob, in the
kingdom of heaven. [12]But the children of the kingdom
shall be cast out into outer darkness: there shall be
weeping and gnashing of teeth. [13]And Jesus said unto
the centurion, Go thy way; and as thou hast believed, so
be it done unto thee. And his servant was healed in the
selfsame hour. [14]And when Jesus was come into Peter's
house, he saw his wife's mother laid, and sick of a fever.
[15]And he touched her hand, and the fever left her: and
she arose, and ministered unto them.

Again and again, we advanced. And again and again, we
prayed and listened. That short trip to the village cemetery
seemed to never end.

We passed through the cemetery's archway entrance. Again
the priest prayed.

Our Father, who art in heaven,
Hallowed be thy name.
Thy kingdom come.
Thy will be done on earth, as it is in heaven.
Give us this day our daily bread.
And forgive us our debts, as we forgive our debtors.
And lead us not into temptation, but deliver us from evil.
For thine is the kingdom, and the power, and the glory,
forever and ever.
Amen.

We listened one last time as his days came to an end. We
lowered him into his grave.

Bazias : Cemetery

01hrs00mins: Checkpoint

Only an hour into the trip, our bus rolled to a stop. To our left sat a guard in his squat guard tower. In front of us, a striped black-and-red steel bar blocked the width of the road. We had no choice but to undergo our first military check. The driver opened the door. The guard officer stepped up the stairs and stuck his head around the corner.

"Anybody appear unfamiliar to you today?" he inquired the driver. He looked toward the passengers in the rear of bus. Satisfied with the driver's answer, he disembarked and waved us on our way. There would be another checkpoint.

Some forty-five minutes later, we stopped again at the next checkpoint. This time, an officer, followed by two guards carrying AK-47s, entered the bus. They stopped at each seat to check identification booklets. Mine had a special red stamp. It indicated that I had been born in a border town. Ludwig's had no such stamp. They inspected him very carefully.

"Where are you going?" the officer asked Ludwig.

"We're going to Bazias." Ludwig motioned toward me.

"He is with me," I elaborated. "We are both going to my grandparent's place on the Danube. Ludwig's father is my supervisor. We are going to get some fish for the celebration of Romania's liberation."

The officer glanced from the booklet to Ludwig then back to me. He handed Ludwig his ID booklet and told us to check into the military base once we got to Bazias. Agreed, he continued to the next row of seats. Although we had passed this test, a distinct but controlled sense of panic set in. I considered what could be in store for us at the third checkpoint. I had passed there several times before on my own. I knew they would be even more apprehensive and distrusting of two young men traveling toward the border together.

A couple of hours passed as the bus continued on its course. Through the dusty windows, I could see fields of green and gold and small villages off in the distance. Small plumes of smoke rose from compost piles. Further across the valley, a quilting of vineyards lie on the slopes of the tree-topped hills. Overhanging tree branches whipped at the bus as it passed. Overhead, the sky was gray with windswept clouds. A breeze was allowed to enter only through partially opened windows, making the ride just bearable on this hot summer day.

God Winks Change Our Destiny

Those last few hot, humid October days made my stay in our three-room house even less pleasant. With nothing to do, and very little to eat, Mom and I checked the level of the Danube together three times daily. It was all we could do to put some normality back into life. Besides, it gave us a chance to talk, weep, and, most importantly, remember.

* * * *

Dad told me that he got the mark on his face when he was a boy. He had found a gun while on a walk in a nearby forest. While cleaning it free of dirt, leaves, and moss, he noticed some markings that looked to be German. He presumed that the gun had been lost during WWII. It took him a little longer to free the trigger. The hammer and the bolt had rusted in the weather. But once they were free, he found that a bullet was still in the chamber.

With the curiosity of a young boy, he reloaded the bullet and aimed at a tree. It was the first time he had actually shot a gun by himself. *Bang!* His right ear throbbed, and his eye went blurry. The gunpowder stung his eye, and the hot cinders burned his right cheek, leaving that appreciable life mark.

* * * *

At night, the Danube shimmered from the light of the moon, the stars above, and the dim streetlights in Yugoslavia.

* * * *

Boy was I happy. My report card from my final grade school placed me number one. Mom was happy too, and Dad was oddly proud too.

"So, son, what are you going to do now? Are you ready for high school?"

After thinking for a moment, I said, "No, I don't think so, Dad. I think it's better for me to go to professional school in Timişoara. I'll get good training there and a chance for a career too."

I really did think that was the best choice anyway. Money was pretty scarce back then. Bazias offered very little, except for the farm commune, the corner store, or fishing on the Danube. Dad was lucky to get the government contract monitoring the level of the Danube. I'd make some money too going to professional school, and it wouldn't add to Dad's worries either.

He smiled and petted my head.

* * * *

On my last evening in Bazias, alongside the Danube, Mom and I talked as she measured the water. Kneeling down, she remembered getting a letter from a student nurse in Oraviţa but forgot just where she had placed it. When we got back to the house, my curiosity brought me to dig around in one of Mom's drawers. Behold, there was the postcard. It read:

September 10, 1979

Doamna Rain,

I met Mr. Rain this morning on my rounds at the hospital in Oravita. Mr. Rain implored me to write you. He has fallen very ill and will be transferred from Oravita to either Resita or Timisoara. I am a student at the nursing school here and can be reached at the following . . .

Regards,
Dumitru Ofelia

Intrigued, maybe this Ofelia knew some of the details about my father's stay in Oraviţa. I thought about visiting her on my way back to Timişoara but thought that might be inappropriate. Before snoozing off to sleep, I wrote her a letter, which I later deposited in Timişoara.

* * * *

The first year of professional school sure turned out great. I really enjoyed the big city and all its distractions, but I kept on the straight and narrow most of the time. Volleyball and soccer and studies kept me busy. I made the top team that first year. Dad thought that was great; and my teachers really pushed me to be a leader, be true and well kept, and not become a trickster.

Dognecea

Ofelia (reading the letter from Doru)

> October 12, 1979

> Dear Dumitru Ofelia,

> I would like to thank you for writing that letter for my father back in September. My mother and I were able to see him for one last time before he died in Timisoara. Apparently encephalitis took his life.
> I am now asking your permission to visit with you sometime in the near future so that I may thank you more personally.
> I await your response with thankful anticipation.

> Yours truly,
> Rain Dragutin

I showed the letter to Mia, my best friend and coworker. As she read it, I asked, "Why would this guy want to meet with me? What do you think, Mia? Should I write him back?" I thought this guy is probably some weirdo. "I don't think I will. What can I do for him?"

"Oh, who knows, Ofelia? Maybe it'll help him get over the death of his father," Mia said.

"Do you think so? I don't really have anything to tell him. I only saw his father once and wrote a letter to his mother. How could I possibly help?" I asked.

"Maybe the guy just wants to say thank you and close the life of his father. It can't hurt you," Mia countered convincingly.

"Well, maybe you are right," I conceded. "I'll just keep it short and tell him to write me back to confirm a date."

Resita : Ofelia and Coworker In Uniform

* * * *

Just a few days later, I was glad to see that Ofelia responded so promptly to my letter. She didn't say an awful lot, but I didn't really blame her. She didn't know me from Adam. In my second letter, I wrote more about myself and suggested a meeting date. I was surprised by how quickly Ofelia responded again and even more curious as she wrote more about herself as well. Maybe we would hit it off.

When the bus arrived in Oravița, it was still very early in the morning. A few people were out and about, so I asked the first person who looked to be a local for directions to the nursing school. Oravița isn't all that big anyway, but the directions helped to find it faster. To my dismay, the building was dark. There was no one near the entrance. Fortunately, the door wasn't locked, so I went on inside. Everything was eerily quiet as I peered down the hallway. There wasn't even a security guard on rounds. I opened the first door on the left, and to my shock and surprise, I stood before a room full of women sleeping in their dormitory. No one stirred, thank God, as I backpedaled my way out the door.

I can't stay here, I fretted. Surely anyone would think the worst if they found me skulking about the dormitory corridors. I quickly but quietly returned to the main entrance. There, a security guard finally came down another hallway. Of course, as I suspected, he was shocked to find me inside. I stated my business matter-of-factly. He told me to return a little later around 9:00 a.m. after the nurses had eaten.

Resita : Ofelia and Doru

With nothing else to do but wait, I left the building. I saw a stand across the road. I drank coffee and ate a piece of dry bread and read the paper.

Ofelia

Oh shit! I slept in this morning a little. I wonder if Doru has come by already. I ran down the hall. I was still in my nightgown. I asked the security guard if a young gentleman had inquired about me. My heart pounded, I think only in part from the run. The guard said that a young man had indeed been here earlier and that he would return after breakfast.

I was so excited. I don't know why. I hadn't even met or talked to him yet, but he sounded so nice in his letters. I hoped Mia was right.

"What do you think I should wear, Mia?" I asked.

"Oh, put on those nice black pants and that new sweater you just bought. They look really great on you," Mia said.

"Do you think so?"

"Oh, if you're lucky, he'll be a looker too! If not, you've got nothing to lose. He'll know you are a great gal anyway," Mia commented.

I put on my makeup, thinking about our first meeting. What a crazy thought. My heart skipped a beat. I didn't feel like myself at all. I was really excited. At the same time, I worried that I would be let down, and our meeting would be just as I expected.

Down the hall in the lobby, I could see a young man talking to the guard. He had black, flowing hair, and he wore the nicest pair of jeans and a strange pair of cowboy-style boots. I wondered if he had bought them in Hungary or Serbia. Before I caught his attention, I ran my fingers through my hair one last time. I patted down my pants and tugged on the sleeves of my shirt. I was ready.

As I approached, Doru turned and smiled at me. He had a wonderful smile. Before I had the chance, he introduced himself.

He thanked me for taking the time to visit with him. I felt his beautiful brown eyes as they glanced at mine and the rest of my body, as he checked me out. I couldn't help but do the same. Those jeans and how they fit so nicely really caught my attention.

After the traditional kisses on the cheek, Doru introduced himself. "I am Rain Dragutin. If you like, call me Doru. All my friends call me Doru. You must be Ofelia. I am glad to have come to thank you for being so kind to my father."

He went on to tell me about his family and where they were from . . .

Doru was born on the banks of the Danube River in the small hamlet of Bazias. Bazias gained some of its notoriety from its monastery that was originally built in 1225. The story goes that the Serbian bishop Sava became land bound here during a boat trip to the east. The winds from the southeast (known as Cosava) blew strongly as they rounded the hills of Serbia. Instead of fighting the wind, the boat was forced to land in this little mountainous cove. There, they stayed for some weeks until the winds subsided. The wind was loud, and Savvas was heard saying, in Serbian, *bas-zias* (noisy wind), which became its name. In that time, they constructed a small monastery.

In 1847, the terminus of the first train route in Romania was completed in Bazias. The route originated in Anina, a coal-mining town in the mountains. It passed westward to Oravița and eventually into Serbia. The tracks then turned south and stopped in Bazias. There, the Danube was deep enough to load the coal onto ships for further transport by boat.

Doru's father and grandfather were born there as well. They were of Serbian descent as were most of the remaining villagers. Serbian was their primary language. His father, Nicolae, worked as a fisherman and a miner. His mother, a Romanian, had a much different story. She was born Viorica Volosniuk in Bucovina with Ukrainian heritage. For some reason, likely due to the massive drought that plagued the area after WWII, Viorica left. She traveled by herself to Bazias. There, she met Nicolae and raised a family. She worked in the only corner store, until the *securitaté* came looking. After an investigation into the finances of the store, she was sent away and served a one-year sentence in one of the harshest jails in Romania. After her detention, the government sent her back to Bucovina. Apparently, she was not legally married to Nicolae, as Doru's last name originally came from her. Later, he changed it to Rain. At that point, his father, Doru, and Nicolae went to Bucovina to reunite with her. They ended up living there for six months. However, Doru's father got into some fights with the Romanians. He was lost there without his Serbian friends. They returned when Doru was four.

Now Doru was nineteen; and he had two brothers, Nicolae, sixteen, and Viorel, two.

Since his father's passing, things become even more difficult. However, his mother was fortunate enough to continue working for the state, monitoring the water level of the Danube. Doru was working in Timişoara to help out his mother. He sent what little extra money he made to her regularly.

The more I learned, the more comfortable I became. He was a real gentleman. In as much as was possible, I felt for him and his loss. It weighed heavy on him, and as much as I tried, I could not find a way to comfort him. Still, I found myself falling ever more deeply for him. I would even say I was in love. But all this while I thought to myself what kind of name is Doru. I had never heard of such a name before.

Before I could interrupt, he was then off again to tell me about Bazias. There was a whole lot of nothing in Bazias. The population was between seventy-five and one hundred. The train tracks had been dismantled. The station had since been dismantled by crooks. The fortress that once stood so proud had fallen into ruins. Each family raised goats, pigs, and chickens to survive. The rich ones kept a cow or two. Besides the corner store and the ancient Serbian Savvas Monastery, the military housed troops there. They patrolled the Danube with a boat and monitored the border.

The military didn't bother anybody in the village. Oftentimes Doru remembered fetching some sweets from the corner store for soldiers behind the encampment walls. Most of the time though, they did regular maneuvers and monitored the road. Typically, the daily traffic consisted of only a very few private vehicles, farmers' horse and trailer, and buses that transported workers from other villages to the mine. At the checkpoint, all vehicles were checked. Any new faces were ordered to produce identification booklets and the reason for their travel. Those without satisfactory reasons were often detained for further questioning.

Other than that, Doru told me that his days as a kid were spent on the Danube swimming, fishing, and watching the tugboats pull their loads up and down the river. The Serbian ships kept to their side, and ours kept to the Romanian side. It was as though an invisible line kept them apart. The bigger boats and cruise ships ignored everything but the channel. They needed to stay in the deepest waters. Oftentimes they came very near the banks near Bazias.

For my part, I told Doru where I grew up as well. Dognecea was much larger than Bazias but still a small village. The best way to describe the place is sleepy. It is a valley village bordered on both sides by mountains forested with deciduous trees. The main road crisscrossed a meandering mountain stream that trickles slowly through it. Houses were built semiattached to the next. They were very near to both sides of the road. So close that few had a front door. You entered the property through the garage gate that opened into a courtyard created by the attachment of the neighbor's home.

My father, Dumitru Alexa, worked in Reşiţa at an industrial plant. My mom, Maria, was a housewife. I had two step brothers—Pavel and Ion—and two step sisters—Iuliana and Gisela—from Mom's first marriage and one brother—Gheorghe. Her first husband died in a mine accident at age twenty-seven.

Mia was right about Doru so far.

* * * *

We spent a good part of the day together talking. She was shy but beautiful to me. She had a special kind of grace. Near the bus station, we sat on the curb. We held hands. Excited, trying not to stare, my eyes dared neither to leave her face nor my hand hers. I kissed her forehead and nose, gently stroking her soft cheeks. Oh, I felt something special for this beautiful young lady. It was sometime before I gave her the chance to tell me about Dad.

Ofelia

As was routine in Romanian hospitals at the time, an entourage of doctors, nurses, and students spent their mornings attending to each patient. I imagine we must have been quite a sight; the doctor always led the way. They always wore a white uniform with a white overcoat. Two nurses dressed in white followed behind him. They then were followed by the four of us student nurses. We wore light blue skirt dresses covered by a white frock in the front to distinguish us.

The morning your father was in the hospital at Oravița was no different. He had a room to himself that lead me to believe that his condition may have been contagious to some degree. Before entering the room, I heard the doctor remark to a nurse that it was odd that his bone marrow was still quite clear; immediately, I guessed encephalitis. My team entered the small room barely wide enough for all of us to pass and then circle back to the door in the same order we entered. There he lay. Doru's father looked to be in his sixties, but I knew from his chart that he was only in his forties. His gray hair added to his frail and weak look. He spoke gently though with clarity to the doctor. The doctor asked him how he was feeling. He took his temperature and told him that he would be transferred to another hospital where specialists could better care for him.

One of the nurses took his blood pressure and noted it in her logbook. The other students and I stood and observed.

Once the brief examination was complete and just as we were leaving the room, your father beckoned the students.

"Miss, excuse me, miss. May I speak to you for a moment?" he called out.

He pointed his finger, and it fell directly upon me. I returned to his bedside. "What can I do for you?" I inquired.

"Can I ask you a favor, please? Can you write a letter to my wife, telling her that I am going to be transferred? Tell her to inform our son Draghi in Timişoara to come and be with me," he pleaded.

"Of course." I assured him that I would do it immediately. I could not refuse this hopeless man and took down his request and address. I bought a card later that morning from the shop on the main floor and mailed it to his wife in Bazias.

* * * *

Before my bus departed, I remarked, "Someday I will marry you."

Danube River Water Levels

04hrs00mins: Naidas: The Path Less Taken

This time, I saw the checkpoint ahead. We had come as far as the village of Naidas where the paved road splits into two; the new paved portion goes to Moldova Nouă and the dirt road to the right to Socol. A semipermanent base camp was set up to the side of the road. Jeeps and trucks were parked in its courtyard. Several soldiers, neatly dressed with automatic guns in hand, manned the barricade. Once we had stopped and the door was open, an officer climbed the stairs, took no notice of the driver, and proceeded to interrogate the first passengers in the front seat. His eyes shifted up and down as he reviewed their IDs. Then he glared toward the rear of the bus. His eyes caught ours. Quickly, I turned and stared out the window. Somehow I felt guilty.

Most of the passengers answered a few questions about where they were going or where they were from as he examined their IDs. With some passengers though, he only gave a precautionary glance at their booklets. Maybe he recognized them from previous journeys.

"Where are you boys from?" he asked.

"Sir, I was born in Bazias, and I am going there to visit my grandparents," I stated in a monotone military fashion. He noticed my red stamp and compared me to my picture. I had aged some since it was taken.

"And you. What is your name?" he demanded.

Ludwig began to explain. He handed the officer his booklet, when I interrupted, reiterating my story about getting some fish for the celebration. He scoffed, took both of our IDs, and continued interrogating others further to the rear. On his return to the front, he passed us by with a cursory glance before departing from the bus. Now what? I hadn't had this happen to me before. He had kept only our IDs; everyone else's, he returned. So there we all sat. Waiting. Sweating. Wondering. Anticipating.

Finally, the officer returned to the bus. I saw him on the phone through a window. I imagined he called someone to discuss our situation with others closer to the border.

"Oh, come on! What's the problem here, officer? I have known them and their fathers since they were boys. Let's get going!" the bus driver snapped impatiently. He was already late.

Somehow persuaded, or at least a little more satisfied, he slapped down our IDs into the driver's hand and shouted back to us. "Be sure to check in at Bazias once you arrive!"

The bus doors folded shut. The driver crammed the stick into gear and gave her a shot of fuel. Again, a black cloud rose from the tailpipe. This time, the smoke blanketed the soldiers at the checkpoint. We sank back deep into our seats, relieved to have made it through all the checkpoints. Ludwig passed me a beer and some bread from his satchel. I tore off a chunk of bread and then toasted Ludwig. More tree branches whipped the side of the bus windows as I glanced ahead toward Yugoslavia. The seat was made of good strong leather, but the road was bad, full of potholes. My back was tight from sitting and bouncing for so many hours.

Guard Tower Overlooking Yugoslavia

* * * *

I had met Ludwig not that long ago. He was a couple of years younger than me, about the same height, five feet eight inches, but heavier set, with dirty blond hair and blue eyes. He had just recently finished his military services. Contrary to my story to the guard, Ludwig wasn't the son of my boss. Both of us worked on the heavy-duty assembly line under the same supervisor. Oftentimes a group of us shared some *ţuică* (Romanian plum brandy) after work before going home. But our mutual relationship really didn't begin until early May of this year.

One evening after work, as we shared a drink, like we did so often before, we found ourselves sitting at a table separated from the others. We were far enough away that we could not be heard. Surprisingly, or so it seemed to me, he reminded me that I had come from the Danube where I had learned to speak Serbian.

"Doru, can I ask you a personal question? Just between the two of us?" he asked hesitantly.

"Sure, Ludwig, what is it?" I guessed that Ludwig might need money or some sort of favor.

"Have you ever thought about how difficult things are here? Well, I've thought about it quite a bit lately," Ludwig said. "Do you remember that guy who used to work across the building? He hasn't been there for some time, you know."

"Ya," I responded, almost questioning.

"Well, rumor is that he escaped to Yugoslavia. The same as the other two guys that we all heard escaped too," he continued on.

I couldn't believe my ears. His conversation was pointing to something that took me totally by surprise. I wasn't his closest friend. That was for sure. My heart raced as I conjectured his roundabout questioning. "All right, Ludwig, stop dancing around the subject. Get to the point," I demanded in a restrained voice.

Ludwig's visage became pronouncedly more serious. In an almost indiscernible whisper, he said, "Well, I want to escape from Romania. I wonder if you had ever considered . . ."

"Shhh!" I caught Ludwig before he could finish his question.

"Hey, this isn't the right place to discuss something like that. I don't really want to talk about that sort of thing," I told him. Obviously, he had earlier concluded that I knew the area well and wouldn't be suspected of such an act. Ludwig took a giant step of faith for him to be so forward. Others from our work had gone missing, and we assumed they had escaped. However, there were so many people that were informants for the secret police that you couldn't guess who was and wasn't. You had to be especially careful with those you hadn't known for a very long time. Ludwig fell into that category for me.

"No, really, I must ask you. You don't understand," he said, looking around at the others nearby. "I will pay you to take me there."

I was taken aback, unnerved by his forthrightness. I told him not to discuss this with me again. I needed time to assess the situation, to see if the risk was worth the reward. This might be the right and perhaps final opportunity for me. Liviu was already five years old and wouldn't yet understand my departure. Ofelia, Ofelia. What would she think? I'd never discussed anything of the sort with her before. And my other buddy, Jivita Radoievici, with whom I'd planned in the past, continued to make excuse after excuse not to go. I needed to think this through. It took me several days to come to a conclusion. I needed to plan how and when first. Most importantly, I needed to be sure that I could trust Ludwig before I approached him.

For the next three days, I saw Ludwig constantly at work. Neither of us made further mention of our conversation. It seemed he was very serious and took my heed not to discuss it further. Could I trust him? On the third day of the afternoon shift, when fewer people were about, I cornered him alone during break time. Lighting a cigarette, I told him I had considered his proposition.

"Ludwig, if I hear or even think that you are going to fuck me, you'll find yourself dead on a street someday," I warned him.

"No, shit, no. I am very serious," he returned. "I've been looking for someone who could speak Serbian and who came from the border area. I'd even pay you to take me if that helps. I have relatives in Germany. We could immigrate there."

My mind a little more at ease, I told him that we would go soon. I had a date in mind, but we needed a detailed plan first. "Can you swim?" I asked him straight-out. He hesitated for a second but then nodded. I was concerned, wondering if in fact he could or if he was just going along unknowingly. Fortunately, he was younger than me, maybe in a good-enough shape to make the distance. This could be my opportunity to have someone along, someone who could hopefully help financially too.

Several weeks and secretive conversations passed before we skipped out early from work to catch the bus to the nearby dam. I wanted—no—I needed to see him swim. I needed to be sure. That particular May afternoon was quite hot when we arrived. I got down to my swimsuit and dove in easily. The water was cool. I swam out a little bit, enjoying the water. Ludwig stood there, still, in his swim shorts, waiting. I shouted to him to join me, but still, he stood. I swam back closer, only to hear him explain that he could swim but not as I had just done. Not fully understanding what he meant, he added that he could swim and was not afraid of the water; however, he had never learned nor practiced an overhand stroke. I told him that was OK now; but for the next month, most afternoons, we would both have to prepare.

It took some time for Ludwig to become a better swimmer than that first afternoon. We were both getting in better shape too. That gave me some confidence. I felt much more positive about our outcome. Personally, I was never bothered about the swim across the Danube. It would be difficult, but I was confident about my swimming abilities. The rest of the trip across Yugoslavia worried me more.

On one of our swimming lessons in early July, we came across some coworkers. They were surprised to see us. But they were not as surprised as we were to see them on our clandestine date.

"So this is what you guys have been doing every afternoon," they stated.

"No. We've only been here a few times, enjoying the water," I lied. And that was the end of that. They didn't question us any further on it, but it sure made me take notice that we needed to be more careful. Luckily, our tool building at work covered that a little too. We had just begun to make some tools to help us install my new hardwood floor.

It was really difficult to make ends meet. We had money, but there was nothing to buy. Most goods of any worth were traded on the black market. My niche was making antennae for households to get illegal broadcasts of Serbian TV. It seemed odd that although most of the apartments were covered with them, attached at irregular angles on every available space, there were so few crackdowns on their use.

Work afforded me the tools and the steel rods and plating to make them. Certainly, it was necessary to hide the extras from the supervisor. He generally turned a blind eye as long as you didn't blatantly show what was going on. It was cheap, with plenty of upsides. Finding customers to barter with wasn't my biggest issue. I had to transport the steel via public transit.

I devised a scheme of how to keep them a minimal length of about one and a half meters. I wrapped them in blankets to keep them somewhat hidden. There is always a cost for any enterprise as I found out. One day, after several journeys on the bus, the driver said that I was no longer able to carry such large items on the bus.

"It is government policy not to transport large loads," he said. I thought to myself this was bullshit as everyone else had bags of materials with them.

"What have you got there?" he asked. "You've been bringing the same-looking thing for some several weeks now. And I just happened to notice."

I looked at him, as straight-faced as possible, but it was clear what was up. He wanted one, whatever it was. He had me at a real disadvantage. This bus was my only ride home from work and to a lot of my clients along the way. So I decided to tell him. "I've got a TV antenna."

"Oh ya! Is it one of those that you can get the special news with?" he asked.

"*Da*. It works pretty well too." I thought that if I elaborated a bit, I could barter with him for free rides. Maybe he'd even add to my clientele. And sure enough, it worked. I installed one at his apartment, and from then on, we had a nice little commerce of trade for food and other stuff.

And that's what we did right up until last week before installing the hardwood.

* * * *

Holy shit! How could I forget that there was one more checkpoint at the border village of Zlatita? The village was so close to Yugoslavia that I could throw a stone over its fence from where we were stopped. Memories flooded back to me, and an anxiousness I cannot explain.

Looking at the fence, it was different now, only about one and a half meters high. Now that I remembered this checkpoint, the fence used to be three and a half meters tall, with circular razor wire at the top. Caricatures of Tito wielding an axe, "The Butcher of Yugoslavia," warned of the brutalities on the other side. Why had it changed? Was it some sort of reflection upon Romanian-Yugoslavian relations? Still, the area in front of the fence was just as I remembered. It was clean. In fact, the dirt was still immaculately raked such that you could see if a bird had walked there, let alone footprints from someone attempting to escape.

Something else was missing too. Oh yes. The flare sites had been removed. Was the trip wire still there though? I couldn't tell from the dusty bus windows. This was tempting. It must be easier to cross here now. Tempting. What am I thinking?

* * * *

Graduation was a day away, and Dad and I were in a bit of a snag. He wanted to see my final grades; I didn't have a formal graduation. It was a good excuse for him to see if he could buy a few things from the big city and then go home. However, for whatever reason, my grades weren't to be posted for another day. That made his stay very awkward. We had nowhere to stay and little money to pay for a room. He couldn't stay in my dorm room either as those were the rules. We decided to stay the night down at the train station. It was the warmest place around, and there were several benches to lie on. Unfortunately, the guards kicked us out every so often to clean, or so they said.

In the morning, we found my grades were posted. Dad was very proud. But I felt that I could have done better. With that done, we wandered the streets, looking to see if any stores had goods. They were pretty sparse. We found nothing we needed. That led us to going back to the train station early and waiting a few hours for our train. Just on our way, a younger boy from a neighboring town stopped us. He was quite upset. His father had not made the trip to Timişoara to pick him up. They didn't have the money, and neither did he, to return home. Stuck here, we were his last chance to get home.

Dad felt sorry for the young lad and checked his wallet for ticket fare. He had enough for the train ticket, but it would mean that we would be short on the fare from Oraviţa.

"Don't worry, we'll get you home one way or another," Dad said to the boy. Dad turned to me and said, "We'll just have to catch a ride from Oraviţa. That's all."

The train ride was boring as usual. It was cramped and uncomfortable. I was glad when it finally stopped in Oraviţa. However, I was surprised by how few vehicles there were that afternoon in Oraviţa. All the passengers scattered. They walked in all directions to destinations seemingly unknown. No one was there to pick anyone up with a vehicle. In our direction though, out of town, no vehicles, not even one truck, could be seen going our way. Instead of mulling about the station, we too joined the others, walking down the road. It looked as though we would walk home. It was only forty kilometers, I might add. Both of us were sure, at least I was very hopeful, that a ride would come our way.

We walked and walked and continued to walk. Behind us, the cement block buildings faded into the horizon. My feet were so sore, my mouth was parched, and my belly rumbled with emptiness. I was happy when we finally got to the third checkpoint in Nidas. It was late by then. The sun was on its final setting, and it wouldn't be long before total darkness would set in. The officer at the checkpoint thought we were crazy and told my father so. How could a man and two boys have walked so far? We had no other choice. The officer didn't want us to continue on so close to the border, but Dad was very insistent about getting home. I had other ideas. Fortunately, before he allowed us to carry on our way, we filled ourselves with water. The soldier had a small snack that he shared with us.

The sun fell quickly; it got very dark. There wasn't a single house light that I could see for some distance. And when the fog rolled in, it was a stretch to even see Dad's outline leading the way in front of us. We followed the crunching of stone under his footsteps. It was eerie.

"*Halt!*" snapped a voice out from the blackness. Startled, my arms dropped to my side. They felt nearly lifeless, beyond my control. I nearly dropped to me knees.

Quickly, Dad replied, "Friend looking for no trouble."

I heard the striking of a match. The spark instantly illuminated the face of a soldier. I could tell that his weapon was pointed directly at us. He was armed and prepared use it. He demanded to see our booklets. Once satisfied, we were left to go on our way again back into the blackness.

Again and again, soldiers stalking in the night stopped and interrogated us. How many more we had missed, or how many had allowed us to pass, I cannot imagine; but it was clear that the border was well protected.

We walked the entire forty kilometers home. Not a vehicle passed to give us a ride.

* * * *

We must stick to our plan! *It is too dangerous here*, I thought to myself. I know the area better on the Danube. Maybe this was some kind of trick with soldiers stationed even more regularly than previously. No. We couldn't take the chance of coming face to face with a soldier. Surely a gunshot at that range would be the end! But what if there wasn't anyone? We could make it quick. I measured the fence. We could leap straight over it without stopping! No, no, no. Stay to your resolve. You grew up in Bazias; there won't be anyone there to catch us for sure! Tonight we must swim across the Danube.

* * * *

But her body in the murky water haunted me still. She was facedown. Lifeless. The start of a clear blue day had turned black. The wind whipped up. The sky was filled with black clouds. It was an ominous scene.

A chain was strapped around her left foot and the other end to a branch. That was all that kept the Danube from taking her. The white meaty back of her arms buoyed on the waves. They appeared to fight, helplessly though, straining to help her find breath. It wasn't to be. Mom was dead. I could barely look. I stood in the water. My legs were limp with fear, powerless. The waves of the Danube crashed upon us as if mad. My stomach ached. Before I forced myself to turn away, to never to look upon her again, Mom's body turned violently. Her arm was outstretched, and she appeared to look right at Ofelia and me. She appeared to beckon us for help.

Ofelia took my hand and led me away from the scene. The military stayed to guard her body. We would have to wait another day before the doctor would arrive to perform the autopsy. I thought with disgust, disdain, and disbelief that it would be so long that my mother laid there waiting for the doctor, barely floating, and likely being scraped by the bottom of the Danube. The chain that kept her there chewed upon her ankle. I prayed that her soul had left, and she was in the good place.

Mom : Rain Viorica

The next morning, Ofelia and I went back to the scene. The doctor laid his black leather bag on the bank. He opened it to prepare for what I could not bear to witness. Again, I turned away and went a little ways back up the hill to the abandoned railroad. I paced back and forth, chain-smoked Carpati, and glanced back occasionally at the horror. All the while, Ofelia braved the matter as a witness.

* * * *

Ofelia

The doctor prepared his satchel. He removed several cutting instruments. I realized then he was about to perform an autopsy right now, right here, among the cattails. Two military men, directed by the doctor, unlocked her foot from the chain. They brought her to the shore. They laid her lifeless, pallid, scraped body on her back directly in front of us.

The doctor began his examination. He noted her appearance in a small notebook. He asked me if I could identify her as Rain Viorica. I nodded in the affirmative. Her eyes were wide open. Yet I feared to look at them. Quickly, after an inspection, the doctor closed them. Her throat was devoid of water and mud as might be expected. He then examined the blackened bruising on her neck. And he noted the cuts on her left ankle. It was all quite overwhelming even for me though I had been trained as a nurse. I felt sorrow for Doru.

Before the doctor could begin, he instructed me to remove her blouse. I delicately unbuttoned her shirt. I tried not to break any threads. This made it all the more terrible and horrifying as he began to cut. First, his scalpel went through the layers of skin, then fat and muscle, to get down into her chest cavity. I maneuvered myself around. My back shielded Doru and the other onlookers from Viorica. I saw the doctor reach for the bone saw. I was aghast at what lay before me. But I am sure that not even my body could hide his sawing motion. I heard the others gasp upon the final chilling cracking of the solar plexus bone. The doctor had to rip it apart to reveal Viorica's inner chest cavity. I caught myself at the edge of nausea and fainting. I prayed Doru could not see.

About his business, the doctor noted some distress to her heart and pointed it out to me. He then looked quickly at her lungs. As her throat, they too were absent of water and mud. My training really seemed to fail me now as I pondered the cause of death. To me, the scene pointed toward drowning. The common lack of water suggested otherwise.

At that point, apparently satisfied with his work, he pushed her chest plate together and motioned to me that the autopsy was complete. There, I was left alone. Thankfully, trained as a nurse, I used the doctor's needle and thread and sewed her back together as best I could. That completed, I buttoned up her now bloodied blouse. I hoped it could hide the horror of the past moments. The doctor thanked me for my help. He explained that he felt she must have suffered a heart attack. Thereafter, she must have fallen into the Danube. Plausible perhaps but too quickly arrived at by the lack of evidence.

* * * *

The bus door swung open, and in stepped the officer. *Stay calm. We can get through this again*, I told myself.

"There are only locals onboard," the driver told the officer. "We were just thoroughly checked back in Naidas."

"OK then, off you go," the officer responded and stepped back off the bus.

What luck! Calm yourself, Doru. Just relax. But how could anyone relax on this part of the road: potholes, ruts, and dust. Dust pervaded every nook and cranny. We closed the windows back in Naidas, but it was already too late. Dust hung in the air, came into my nose and lungs, and settled upon my clothes. Now, for sure, we had nothing to do but sit and wait for this part of the journey to end in Socol.

07hrs30mins: Socol: Friends Along the Way

August 18, 1979, 5:30 p.m.: The squeal of the bus's breaks shocked me back into reality. I realized we were in Socol. Only seven kilometers remained on our journey home. Still, I had no intention of making it by foot as some of the others did. Besides, I knew that another transport carrying miners would pass by. Furthermore, one bicycle ride with Dad reminded me too . . .

* * * *

I studied even harder the second year of professional school. I was elected to the important post of secretary of the youth organization. I organized all sorts of activities and was a key player on the soccer team. I became quite close to my teacher. We spent considerable time together during and after school and most times on the weekends. He was really knowledgeable about politics in particular. We read quite often together and in our special group from our little red book.

Strangely, I was disappointed to leave the school year behind. I really enjoyed it. Still, I was excited to see Dad, Mom, and Viorel. What was I going to do all summer in Bazias? Work on the collective farm?

* * * *

All my grade school friends were playing soccer. And Viorel and I sure wanted to play as well. We were good players. Instead, we were piling rocks!

Dad and Mom, and my uncle's family, worked up the hill in the forest. They were digging rocks out of the cliff near the top. The big ones, they pushed them down the hill toward us. We had to help carry the smaller rocks from the top. Most times we first threw them down as far as we could. That was kind of fun.

Next to the road, our pile of rocks grew. Dad instructed us to arrange them into rectangles, four meters long, two meters wide, and one meter high. All the while, he pounded the larger boulders with a sledge hammer. He used a wedge, placed into the cracks, to split them into smaller pieces.

The villagers from Socol came by truck, or horse and buggy, to take them back to the village. They used them to reconstruct house foundations.

All this, Dad said, was to help feed the family. It was hard work.

* * * *

I got the opportunity to go to summer school for two weeks. All my buddies were going too. How would Dad take it, though, because I needed money for the trip? Summer school was only two weeks after I got home. Mom didn't really help when I broke the news to her. She told me to go fishing with Dad.

So fishing we went one evening. It sure was dark. There wasn't a moon that night, and the Danube was so murky. Fortunately, the fish were biting.

"Dad, I've been asked to go to youth camp this summer," I mentioned in passing.

"Are you planning on going?" he asked.

"I'd like to, but it starts in another week."

"Are you sure this is for you? Do you think it will be good for you?" he questioned me.

I put another worm on my hook and cast out into the Danube. The bobber bounced up and down before being slowly swept along by the current.

"I'm not sure, Dad. But I would like to go see for myself what it is all about," I finally replied.

We caught a dozen fish that Dad was lucky enough to sell in town. We went back every night for almost the entire week before Dad decided on a new fishing hole. It was six kilometers downstream toward Divici.

I jammed my buttocks between the handlebars, the fishing string in my pockets, bag, bait, and hooks in hand. Dad pushed off, swerved to the left and then to the right as we started, then peddled our way down that damn road. Every bump bruised my ego and my ass. My arms hung like lead, and my hands fell asleep as I tried not to fall off. We had better catch some fish.

The partial moon showed itself a bit this evening. Several massive boats went by. It seemed too dark for this time in the evening. Dad stopped the bike with little notice. We were here. I couldn't tell why he picked this spot. It all looked the same to me. We fashioned two rods from willow with our pocketknives. Crouching, we cast out the lines time and time again. Nothing, we didn't even get a damn nibble. One hour, two hours passed, still nothing. It was getting darker now. Sirens sang in the north, and we could see the spotlights scan the open landscape. Dogs barked in the distance. And we still didn't get a bite.

I had had enough of this. Dad did too, I think, as his line had gone limp; and he struggled to pull it in without bunching the line.

"Ah, the line's dead," he exclaimed.

But the line came taught and kept creeping toward him.

"Got a log?" I asked.

Then the line went taught and pulled in the opposite direction of the stream. Dad let the line out steadily but not too quickly. The spool whirred as the line lengthened. He must have something big! I rushed to take off my pants. I crawled into the murky water with net in hand. The bottom mud oozed through my toes as I slid quickly up to chest height in the water. It was deeper than I thought. I tossed my shirt onto the bank. I could smell the rotten bottom plants as bubbles formed on the surface. The line wasn't far from me now. I reached out searching for the line. A whiskered black head showed itself just below the water.

"Now don't miss with that net when I get him close to you. We might only get one chance at it," Dad said softly as though not to warn the fish. But he couldn't hide his excitement.

Steady. Steady. I curled my toes into the mud to get a good stance. Then there it was. I leaped and missed. I couldn't believe it. Our only chance at a single fish, and I screwed it up. Ah!

Oh, but back again, it struggled, shaking its whole body, still attached to the line.

Steady. Steady. Get a grip. Swooshing, down came the net, and in it went the beast. Water splashed onto my face, filling my eyes, nose, and mouth. The water tasted black. But I dug deeper into the mud. I curled my arms and with all my might flung that fish out of the water, against the bank, into Dad's hands. It was flopping like mad. I scurried back onto the bank. There was a strong wooden branch there. I used it to smack the fish on its head.

It was huge catfish. Bigger than any I'd seen before. How were we going to get this monster back to Bazias? With both hands, Dad took it over to the bicycle. He put his right hand thumb in its mouth. It protruded through its gills. He strangled its tail with his left. He marched it back to the bike and slipped the handlebars through its gills. Great idea. It was so long its tail flopped onto the ground. On the walk back to Bazias by the light of the moon, we talked and joked. Across the blackness of the Danube, the light of homes and streetlights flickered.

Thirteen kilograms! Dad sold it for 130 lei. That was enough and then some to pay for the ride, a pair of sneakers, and a new toothbrush!

* * * *

The ride to Timişoara was as uneventful as usual. I passed the time admiring my new shoes, pondering the prospects of summer school. Oddly though, I didn't know who else was going to be there, and the teachers gave me little information about what we would be doing or studying. Still, I was very excited to be away from home and the chores of the summer crops.

My excitement soon turned to curiosity and somewhat to dismay when we all gathered at the predetermined meeting place in Timişoara to get transport to the camp. We were all boys! I was expecting and hoping for something more akin to the ratio of boys and girls at professional school. I thought maybe if I hoped enough that girls would somehow already be there or they would come from other locations.

My hopes were dashed once we got to the country retreat.

* * * *

Pera got off the bus before us. I could see him standing outside waiting for us.

"Doru, listen. Come to my home and say hello to my wife. I've got some good homemade *ţuică* we can share while you're waiting," he proclaimed. So we did.

His house was only a short walk from the bus station. There, his wife greeted us with outstretched arms; and we shared kisses to the cheek, first to the right then to the left. She sat us down at the lone table in the middle of the kitchen and fed us some dried fish and roasted and pickled peppers. Pera poured us a shot of *ţuică*.

"*Noroc!* It has been some time since we last saw you. I am glad to see you are doing well," he raised his shot glass, and we drank. Pera told us about his visit with his son who was now an engineer.

As the time passed, I recounted a time at school in Socol when I went to dig for worms.

* * * *

"You know, it was just down the road from here when I had the strangest thing happen to me back in grade school," I hesitated for a second. Maybe I shouldn't recount this tale. But it was too late now, I thought.

The principal asked me how the fishing was on the Danube. I imagine he had thought about it before. Should he, a member of the communist party and a leader of the community, be caught, it would most certainly damage his career. I told him that I had had some luck.

In any event, he was going fishing at another place that night and asked me to get some worms for him. He gave me a bag and a shovel and directed me to the bank of a small creek where the earth was damp. He was right. The earth was damp, rich, brown, and full of worms as I dug. It even smelled rich and musky like mushrooms in my hands as I plucked them.

"Pst!" A voice from behind startled me. I stopped digging for the worms. There was a man wearing a soldier's uniform. He called over to me from across the little Nera creek. "Hey, come over here." He was a Yugoslavian soldier. He waved, bidding me come across the border. "It'll be OK. Life is better here. I'll take care of you."

* * * *

My glass was empty. Pera poured me another. I didn't understand back then. This was how I grew up. I didn't know any better. I was too young to understand what he was alluding to.

Seven o'clock in the evening came quickly upon us. We needed to take our leave. We drank to health over one more shooter. We shook hands and shared a hug. "Please stop by on Monday to visit us. *La revedere. Drum bun.*" Pera said goodbye and wished us a good trip.

As I turned away from Pera, I immediately recognized a figure of a passing military officer. I remembered him distinctly from my childhood days in Bazias.

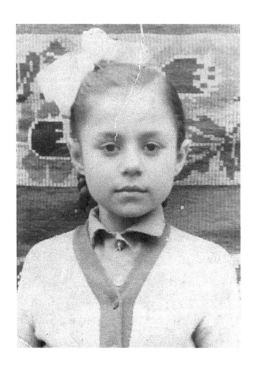

Rain Ofelia as a Young Girl

Ofelia's Class Photo

Resita: Liviu's Class photo

Socol : Doru's Class Photo

Military Service—UM 01256

Not long after my first meeting with Ofelia in Reşiţa, I had to report in for conscription to one-year mandatory military service. Up to that point, Ofelia and I kept in regular contact. However, I was in Timişoara, and she was mostly in Reşiţa. We talked on the phone when practicable. Her work's phone was the only one available to her. That wasn't ideal. I sent lots of mail too, telling her how I felt and how I hoped she would wait for me to finish my military service.

Fortunately, Ofelia was able to visit me several times before I left. She had to go to nurse training in Arad. She made it a point to stop in and stay for a while.

I was eventually stationed in the southern village of Caracal—UM 01256. It was an artillery base located just on the northeast outskirts of Caracal. The base covered an oddly shaped area. Its dimensions were about five hundred meters east to west and one kilometer north to south. A cemetery, Cimitirul Eroilor, sat on the west side. We shared our practice range, just north of it, with UM 02529. A railway bordered us to the east and wrapped around us to the north. The main entrance for vehicles was on this side in between the base and the train yard, though most foot soldiers entered and exited down Strada Infratirii in the southwest to get into town. Its buildings were primarily whitewashed stucco covered with pink tile roofs. The barracks were single-story buildings about fifty meters long.

Caracal : Doru in the Military

For the first forty-five days, called *perioda soldatului*, we learned how to march and how and whom to salute. We dismantled, cleaned, and reconstructed our AK-47. Every day, we spent some time cleaning. We cleaned the barracks, we cleaned the beds, and we cleaned our military bags. We were housed in barracks that held forty-eight men each. Mine was the second in a line of four, very near to the terminus of Strada Infratirii. There were a dozen or so barracks full of soldiers in training. A single wood-fired heater kept us warm. There was a single TV. And there was a single channel to watch, one day per week—Saturday night. We got quite proficient at fixing the antenna to get Bulgarian football.

Each morning we were grouped into a team of six men. We had to push the canon to the field. One man led with the barrel on his shoulder. A second man sat on the barrel to distribute the weight. The remaining four soldiers pushed from behind.

The field was about one kilometer away down a dirt road. Each of us learned how to maintain, load, aim, and fire the canon.

After forty-five days, all barracks men assembled in the field. We had to take an oath to be loyal to Romania. We had to fight to the end!

With that, the *perioda soldatului* ended. I was selected to go to school to become a sergeant. It lasted for three months of the first half of the military time. It was difficult. It was all memorization. We were kept together in a different dormitory just for those in this special training. Upon my return to base camp, it seemed like all we did was guard stuff and places and practice to shoot the weapons.

We were then separated into batteries. Each battery had four canons. Each group of six men had to take turns guarding the facility for twenty-four hours. We were given live ammunition— two clips of bullets. Our guard duties started at 3:00 p.m. The officer in charge inspected us before sending us off to our positions.

We began with guarding the base. There were six main points: (1) The entrance, where we checked IDs and reported vehicles leaving and entering the base; (2) the flag, where we marched back and forth; (3) the food deposit and (4) the ammunition deposit, where we kneeled behind dirt; (5) the tower, where we could see the whole base; and (6) a weak point near to a road, where we observed people passing by. Each group stayed in position for three hours. We then returned to the dormitory, for rest and food. I always felt sleep deprived as six men slept in a big bed, fully dressed except for boots.

One day at around 11:45 p.m., I was woken by the dormitory guard on duty. It was my turn for guard duty between 12:00 p.m. and 3:00 a.m. I asked him if anything interesting was happening, and he responded, "*Na.* Quiet. You just need to keep the fire going."

So I dressed myself slowly and rather casually. I slipped on my boots, deciding I didn't need socks for such a quiet time.

Once dressed, I walked a little. I got some air to wake up and then returned to the fire to rest on a small chair. Everyone was asleep. The alarm sounded in the dormitory area. I hadn't heard it before but knew from our training the steps I needed to take. I yelled "Alarm! Alarm! Alarm! Alarm!" so that everyone would wake up. They began to dress and get their guns and gear prepared. In turn, I ran to the commander's house. He lived in an apartment in town. His place was about five hundred meters away down Strada Infratirii and south down Strada Bistritei. It was quite chilly but the run heated me up quickly.

I knocked on his door briskly and informed him that there was an alarm on base. Immediately, he dressed and followed me out into the night. We ran and marched back to the camp.

Back in the camp, it became clear that it was a serious matter. It was not just a false alarm. A three-star colonel from Bucharest had come to participate in a readiness drill with our camp. He stood there watching everyone run about. He continually looked at his watch measuring our readiness. We loaded the trucks with food, supplies, guns, and live ammunition.

Once ready, he gave the order to leave camp and go to the area. We rode on the trucks for about fifty kilometers fully prepared. Once there, we dismounted and placed the canon in its intended spot. There, we waited for the colonel to inspect us. He was very thorough. He was going through backpacks, belts, guns, etc. We were required to have a clean gun. Our bag was supposed to be full of the prescribed amount of articles: green shirt, soap, razor, underwear, two pair of socks, etc.

Eventually, he came to me. He checked my gun, including the barrel. He did a quick salute and then told me to empty the contents of my bag. He checked the soap, the razor, the shirt, and my three pair of socks. He questioned me, "What is going on here?"

"Sir," I responded, "I had to run to get the commander and in the haste neglected to put on my socks."

"Take your boots off," he commanded. They were bare, of course. More importantly, they were red. "Put a pair on now, dammit, before you get frostbite!" he shouted.

As it happened, Ofelia and I were able to keep in touch, though less frequently, with the mail. For us, soldiers, Monday was a great day of anticipation. We received mail this day of the week. Most times I received several letters from Ofelia and my mother.

One Monday, I received a notice from the mailman that I had received money and to come directly to claim it. I wondered who it could be from—Mom or Ofelia is all I could think. And neither of them had any spare money. Off I went to claim my money, in a generally good mood, as I had already figured what I would buy. The mailman asked who sent me the money. Of course, I didn't know yet anyway. "I don't know," I responded. We stood there staring at one another.

Baffled by his comment, I said, "Well, then give to me." Still, we stood there staring at one another. What could he want?

"Who is the money from?" he demanded again. We stared even longer, and I shrugged.

"From my mother, Rain Viorica . . .?" I told him, half asking.

"No," he retorted.

I wondered if this was some sort of Twenty Questions before he would give it to me. It was my money. Why won't he just give it to me then? I asked, "Where is it from then?"

"Resita," he replied hesitatingly.

Who in the hell do I know there? I was just drawing blanks. I stood and stared even longer. "It's from a lady," he finally added.

That shook my memory. Of course, it must be from Ofelia. I told the mailman who, and then he gave it directly to me. Strange.

I went straight to the market and bought some oranges and a few bananas. I longed for fruit ever since I began this mandatory hell.

Ofelia

I was excited this morning. We were going on a road trip to the Danube. I had never been there before, so I was really looking forward to it. The nurses and I piled into the rear of the minibus-style ambulance. The doctor and the driver were in the front, of course. We had a goal this day of collecting one hundred liters of blood from the farmers in the countryside.

We passed through Naidas, where the guardsmen smiled coyly at all us girls in the rear. In Socol, we were asked for our identity cards, of which I had forgotten to bring. They let me be though as it was quite obvious we were stopping here to make a good collection. We were there for about two hours and extracted blood from just about all the locals who were home that day, not out in the collective's fields.

Later in Bazias though, the military were much more formal. They demanded our identity cards. The doctor tried to explain, and certainly, I did too. After some discussion, the private went off to get his supervisor, and I figured I was in some sort of trouble. When he approached, I could tell he meant business; and in a low forthright tone, he demanded, "Where is your identity book?"

I really had nothing new to offer except that I had forgotten it in Reşiţa. Then I remembered! "I know Mrs. Rain. She could vouch for me. I am certain," I said matter-of-factly but with really no certainty at all that she would ever recognize me. We had talked by phone several times, and Doru had only seen me in a picture he had sent some time ago.

"Go get this Mrs. Rain," he demanded of one of the soldiers. It was clear they knew who she was and where she lived as he ran off toward a blue house in the middle of the small village. During our wait, the supervisor scolded the doctor, just out of earshot, for not ensuring his nurses were prepared with the appropriate documents.

Upon their return, Doru's mom, or at least who I presumed was Doru's mom, because I had never seen her before, came directly to me and kissed me on both cheeks before giving me a gentle hug.

* * * *

Every so often, we continued our guard duties off base. There was a huge underground ammunition storage in Pădurea Reşca. It was so well hidden. I am not even sure the locals knew that it existed. In a clearing nearby, there was a cabana reportedly visited by Ceausescu. We had to guard the storage facility for twenty-four hours at a time.

We trained with live ammunition at the training range in Poligonul Redea. We had to drive to get there as it was some fifteen kilometers to the southwest of our base. The area was massive and flat. The field was well mowed; clearly, animals grazed there from time to time. However, we never saw any farmers letting their animals graze in the field. They must have been prewarned to clear the area. My AK-47 was ready for the drills.

Training consisted of three targets, one at about one hundred meters, another at one hundred fifty meters, and the last at two hundred meters. All resembled a human figure. They gave us three bullets for the first target, three bullets for the second, and ten for the farthest. We could not use more than the allotted bullets for the first two targets. If you shot well, then you could use the extra bullets to hit the final fully automatic moving target.

Punishment for not successfully completing the task included push-ups, cleaning, running, and more cleaning!

After the AK-47 came the live canon ammunition practice. Off in the distance was a target in the shape of a tank. It moved as well. For the canon, we had a team of six. One man was on his knees at the ammunition box, and he passed it to another and then to another. The fifth man then loaded the shell into the canon and yells "ready." The sixth man, the shooter, sat behind the canon, aimed, and shot the target. Our shells were fifty-seven millimeters. Other groups had a larger eighty-five-millimeter gun.

"Fire!" yells the commander, and off we would shoot.

We always finished with a barrage! A new case of shells was given to the first man, and all of the regiment fired at will. The noise was deafening.

Ofelia

In November of 1972, Doru finished his mandatory military service. At the time, I lived in the city, sharing an apartment with a colleague from the blood bank. The day he came to see me, I was aghast by how he looked. He had lost so much weight. His eyes were sunken, and his cheeks were drawn tight to the bone. He was pale from malnutrition but in great spirits to see me. My heart just ached to see him so.

I must have been in love, for I longed to be with him so badly. I asked, "Doru, I want to get married right away. Do you love me?" I was only nineteen and he twenty-one, but it was obvious we were made for one another.

Doru smiled his big smile, and his eyes twinkled at me. "Sure, I'll call in to work and get some time off right away."

And so off we went on the bus to my parents in Dognacea. We were greeted as family once we arrived. I had talked a lot about Doru over the past years, and they knew the fondness I felt for him. It showed that they loved him too.

When the time was right, Doru approached them in his special formal manner and asked my parents for my hand in marriage. Of course, they agreed. So it was to be that Doru and I were to be wed in January 14, 1973.

The wedding was as per usual in Romania. We had no special frills. I had my family with me. The sun was warm as we walked down to the town hall. Snow covered the road, and big snowflakes fell from the sky. We were happy. When we arrived at the town hall, the fireplace was stoked, and the smell of smoke was in the air. Of course, Ceausescu's picture hung on the wall behind the mayor's desk.

We all stood there inside the mayor's office; and in the presence of God, Ceausescu's picture, and my family, we were wed in a short communist ceremony. That being done, we walked back the five kilometers that we had just come. The snow was still falling but not so heavy. Few people were on the streets. The two of us, now one, held hands and embraced all the way. We were both quiet, wondering what we had actually done. From time to time, Doru squeezed my hand, just to assure me and him that we would be all right.

At home, we ate a meal, and that was the end of the honeymoon.

Several months had passed when mother asked me if there was a problem. Doru had found a good job at the foundry, I was working, and we had moved in to our new apartment. All should have been well, but Mom being Mom, she knew something was amiss.

"What is it?" she asked. "What troubles you, dear?"

At first, I wanted to deny anything was wrong. She knew though, and I could no longer keep it a secret.

"Do you love Doru?" she asked.

Surprised and angry at the same time, I answered, "Of course. I love Doru very much!"

"Well then, if you love Doru so much, why aren't you happy? I can see it in your face that you are not happy," she told me.

"Listen," I said to my mom. "I do love Doru immensely. But I am not so sure I like what comes with him: the cooking, the cleaning, and the . . ." I stuttered. "And the *sex*!"

Mom's upper body moved backward. A smile came across her face as she relaxed back into her chair. She laughed a wry laugh then said, "Listen to me. Doru is a good man.

"Cooking. You have to learn how to cook your way. Today you put salt, it is too salty. Tomorrow put less salt. Don't worry, you will learn to cook because you both need to eat.

"Cleaning. You are a nurse, for god's sake! Hygiene is a part of you, of who you have become.

"Sex. Give it time. Sex is going to be the best part of your marriage. Believe it!"

09hrs00mins: Socol to Bazias: Calm Before the Storm

August 18, 1979, 7:00 p.m.: That military figure must be of Popovici Stefan. Even from behind, I knew it was him. When we left Pera and his wife, the officer must have been thirty meters ahead. Sure, it had to be him. I remembered he had married a girl who lived on Pera's street as a kid.

We had only walked a few tens of meters when the officer suddenly stopped. The tapping of our footsteps must have alerted him of our approach. As he turned, I could vaguely see his face. The peak of his hat hid his eyes. And as we neared, I was sure it was Stefan.

"Hello, Stefan. How are you?" I asked.

"Doru? Is that really you?" Stefan proclaimed as he recognized me.

"Sure it is. It has been a long time, but you haven't changed too much." He had more chevrons on the shoulder of his uniform. And his hat was adorned with an officer's badge. He had risen to the rank of captain. "It looks like you have been promoted to a good position," I said, pointing at the stars on his arm sleeves on the shoulder of his uniform.

"*Da.* I'm captain of the border region now. How have you been? I heard you have a family now too," he inquired. His chest heaved out; he raised his chin. The proudness flowed from him.

"All is OK. It has become very difficult in Reşiţa, as you know. I got married to Ofelia, and we have a boy, Liviu," I told him.

Turning his attention to Ludwig, he interrogated me. "Who is this guy?"

"This is Ludwig Rorig. He is my supervisor's son. He came with me to visit my grandparents. We are going to buy some fish for the upcoming celebration," I explained.

He continued his interrogation. "How are you getting to Bazias?"

"Oh, we are going to catch a ride with the miner's transport," I explained.

Captain Stefan thought for a moment. "You can accompany me to Bazias." He gestured to go over to his jeep. His camouflaged green jeep was parked over at the mayor's office. Clearly, he left no option other than for us to share the ride.

"Sure, if you want to take us, take us." We accepted his invitation. Awkwardly, Ludwig crawled into the rear of the vehicle. Stefan held the door open while Ludwig offered his hand and pulled me into the rear. Stefan then plopped into the front. With his right hand, he slammed the door shut.

"To the camp in Bazias," Stefan ordered the driver.

The driver flicked his cigarette butt out the window and with his right hand ground the gear into place. We were off as the jeep bounced across the rutted shoulder of the road onto the smoother portion of the narrow main road. Stefan lit a cigarette and passed the pack back to us. For a while, we discussed what we had been doing for the past couple of years. It was just small talk, but it passed the time. On the left, there was a single tall tree. Past it, I briefly saw our small garden plot where my family grew corn. The mountains were getting closer on our left. We were at the end of what probably represented the terminus of the Carpathian Mountains.

The jeep continued up a very gentle rise, and suddenly, there it was. The Danube was straight ahead of us. The road made a sharp turn to the left and continued winding along hugging the mountain's edge. Now to our right, both Ludwig and I were drawn to the window. The railway track was beside us and then the waters of the Danube below it. We could see where the Danube disappeared to the west out of the heart of Yugoslavia. We also peered directly across its incredible width to the smaller hills on the far side. I estimated it was nearly two kilometers across. Billows of smoke rose from the abundance of cargo ships and tugboats pulling their loads. They were likely delivering goods to Ram, Dubovac, and Smederevo. Smoke hung in the air farther off in the distance.

"So did you think it could be so big?" I commented to Ludwig. It had been some time since I had last seen it. Ludwig sat silent, measuring its ominous grandeur and contemplating the task at hand for sure. I was certain he hadn't quite imagined this. He continued to stare out the window.

Right in front of us, the Danube was at its greatest width as it spread out over the plain made by a huge sweeping turn to the south, creating the natural border between Romania and Yugoslavia. In front of us, it continued its journey down to the southeastern extent of Romania where it eventually would pour out its silt-laden load into the Black Sea. The current here is more sluggish, constant, and powerful. Its breadth had increased and its depth increased due in large part to the huge damn to the south in Portile de Fier. Boats, tugs, and ships of all sizes and types with their myriad of cargo required its depth. There were at least twenty that I could count at this time. That's why Mom used to monitor the water depth.

As if on key, Stefan offered, "I am sorry about your mother, Viorica. Her drowning must have been a real shocker for your family."

"Thank you, Stefan. It really was hard to understand. How could she have drowned just checking the water level?" I questioned him.

Stefan asked, "Have you read the newspapers lately? There have been a lot of people attempting to cross the Danube as of late. They are a bad bunch. Some may make it. But rest assured many others are caught by me. Many drown or are swept up by a passing barge." Captain Stefan forewarned us.

"I haven't really paid much attention to it," I answered honestly.

"You guys wouldn't be thinking about trying something, would you?" Captain quipped.

"Of course not." Ludwig and I shook our heads as though in disgust for questioning our integrity. "I told you I've got a wife and my five-year-old son, Liviu, back in Reşiţa." I assured him. I tried to focus on Stefan, but I was distracted by the familiar surroundings. Before we entered Bazias, I looked quickly at the cemetery, searching for where both my mom and dad were put to rest. A tear dropped from my eye as I remembered them both. I was tempted to ask Stefan to let us out there. But I just couldn't.

"I know. But many strangers have tried to cross under my patrol. I am responsible to stop these crazy people from risking their lives. Have you seen any strange persons on your journey?" he inquired.

"No, hell no, just us. We haven't seen anyone," I assured him again. I noticed through the tree branches Grandpa's distinctive baby blue house some one hundred meters on the left.

"Make sure you tell me if you see any strange movements. You never know who is going to try to escape these days," he said. "You guys wouldn't try something like this under my watch now. Right?" he inferred. The driver slowed down as we passed by the monastery and the community center. We could see the checkpoint gate was down across the road.

"Come on, Stefan. You have known me for so long. Why would I try something so crazy now? I'm twenty-eight. I've got a wife and a boy. I'm telling you, I would have tried years ago before all this if I had wanted to leave," I stated.

Laughter, voices, and music from the community center interrupted our conversation as we passed by.

Stefan's interrogation finally ended as the vehicle halted fifty meters further on. The road was blocked. The red-and-white banded gate protruded from the little guard shack. The shack was slightly bigger than a telephone booth. Out stepped a soldier. He immediately saluted to Captain Stefan.

Stefan got out. Ludwig pushed the seat forward, and we clambered out onto the road.

"OK, guys. It was nice to see you. I'll notify the authorities that you are here. Let me know if you see any strange movements. Bye for now." He extended his hand. We shook hands, and then we went off on our separate paths.

09hrs00mins: Bazias: Dancing in the Rain

August 18, 1979, 7:30 p.m.: Saved only by the journeys end, we passed the interrogation. We walked up the main dirt road past the community center. The party was just starting to get lively. We carried on for fifty meters, beyond the monastery, before turning right onto the dirt track toward Grandpa's house.

Stefan was stationed in Bazias when I was a schoolboy there. I guessed he was six years my senior. He had progressed well in his battalion and was given the opportunity to further advance his rank should he choose to stay in Bazias. He also had the option of retiring from his military service and return home near the Black Sea. Apparently, he chose the former. Stefan went on to school. He returned some fourteen years later, this time as captain. I remembered him to be a serious soldier even as a kid. Man, he sure played the part of a true communist now!

Grandma Liubita was the first to greet us at the door. Her hands met my cheeks, and she stared straight up into my eyes. She was examining my every feature as though she had forgotten. She softly pulled my head downward toward hers. She kissed me on the right cheek. Then she kissed me again on my left and back over to the right for one last one.

"Oh, I am so glad to see you, *draghi*!" Her hands were still cupping my cheeks. "Come in. Please, please." She put her hand behind my shoulder, subtly pushing and guiding me inside. I began to introduce her to Ludwig when Grandpa and my youngest brother, Viorel, made their way from the back dimly lit bedroom into the single main living area.

"Oh, my boy. What a pleasant surprise," Grandpa Jivko said. He took my arm and led me over to the table. He bent over so that his lips were closer to my ear. In a soft voice, he whispered, "Did you happen to bring me a bottle of Vermouth?"

"Oh, I forgot, *buni*." My hand covered my mouth. "I'll be sure to find one before I go back to Reşiţa." Winking, I promised him. Viorel too was looking for a present. My watch was all I could think to give him. So I unlatched it from my left wrist and gave it to him. His face grinned. He was happy.

With the introduction complete, Grandma went off to the winter kitchen and returned with a nondescript small bottle of *ţuică* made from plums. She poured each of us men one and then asked if we were hungry. I could smell its strength before we even tasted. Taking the glasses up, we clinked them together in the middle. We saluted one another, "Noroc si sanatate!" Grandma went back again to the kitchen to fetch some fish, bread, and pork fat and, of course, some hot peppers.

We ate a little, talked some more, and drank another shot or two. By now, it was getting a little late, and I wanted to see my uncles Sretko and Zoran before going to the village festival. Before we picked up our bag and other belongings, we shook hands with Grandpa. Grandma gave me another kiss on the cheek. Viorel followed us.

Bazais : Home

Maybe one hundred meters from the community center, we stopped at my uncle's place for a short visit. Music and laughter came louder now from the community center. We were downwind. The noise traveled more freely in our direction as the party was well under way. Ludwig, distracted by the frivolity, glanced continually through the window open to the festivities. He had never visited a small village before, let alone one having a big celebration.

August 18, 1979, 9:00 p.m.: Outside the community center, the flickering of several small bonfires cast shadows upon the nearby monastery. Small groups of friends gathered around each pit, drinking beer, wine, and *ţuică*. Some of the groups were quiet; but most danced, sang, and laughed, enjoying their time together. Popular accordion music sang from within the community center. We were drawn to its frivolity, especially Ludwig, who made a direct motion to the front doors. I stopped at the rear of a parked car. Bemused, and yet somehow horrified, I looked upward as I put my hands together as if praying. I smirked at the sticker of a bare naked lady spread out across its rear window. "Jesuus Christ!"

Cigarette smoke puffed out when we opened the entrance door. It stung my eyes and filled my lungs. The accordion music and laughter also hit us square in the face. All sorts were there. There were whole families, some dressed up fine in their Sunday clothes and others in farm coveralls. Long wooden tables stretched down one side of the hall. Soldiers filled them mostly. On the other side sat people on chairs huddled in private circles. The center wooden floor was crammed with couples dancing to the music of the accordion.

It was an annual event in Bazias for the surrounding village folk to come and celebrate St. Preobrazenie. My eyes fell upon many that I recognized from years gone by. At one of the tables sat many of my school friends. Ludwig and I pushed our way through the crowd to join them.

"Doru, how are you!" They all cheered as we approached. "*Ce faci*? How's it going? Great to see you! What are you doing back here?"

"Just visiting the grandparents. We have come to drink with my school chums!" I proclaimed.

"Who is your friend?" the ladies inquired.

I hugged everyone first. Then I proclaimed that this was my friend Ludwig. We snatched a couple free chairs and sat ourselves at the big table. Immediately, a newly filled glass of wine was pushed toward the both of us. Everyone raised their glasses. *Noroc!* Cheers!

Across from me sat Jivoine. "Hey, what in the hell is that in the back window of your car? Are you nuts?" I asked. We all laughed hysterically.

We all sat laughing, while each took our turn telling stories. I told a few of my own.

"Do you remember when we were back in grade school in Socol, somebody found a chunk of carbide? I can't remember where, but that doesn't matter. Anyway, we all met later that night in Bazias. We mixed the carbide with some water into an old paint can, closed the lid tightly, and then shook it." With my right elbow pointing out, and my left hand holding onto my right wrist, I motioned as though giving a headlock. "I held the can tightly between my chest and arm. *Bang!*" I shouted. It exploded like a shotgun. The lid flew off above. "We did this over and over again. None of the grownups in Bazias seemed to pay attention, so we kept on with it."

"Then, do you remember? Jesuus Christ. To our horror, or maybe just to our stupidity, the Yugoslavians on the other side of the Danube started shooting off tracers into the blackness of the night sky? Jesuus Christ! When that sky lit up, we ran like hell to hide."

Laughter erupted.

* * * *

The odd thing I found about the whole affair though was the next day at school. At around 9:00 a.m., the principal called upon each classroom to gather outside. As we departed from the exit, he separated all the kids from Bazias into a group, except for me. In a scolding fashion, he stood between the two groups. I was at his back. He denounced the actions of the previous night.

"Do you not understand the disgrace you have brought upon this school, upon your family, and upon yourselves? Great disgrace!" he answered his question. "Have we not taught you that your good actions are important for the better good of the community?" He turned and looked at me as if saying to the others that I was the good example. "Your generation will become the strength of the communist party."

My cheeks turned red. We all stood there in disbelief as I was not part of the group; I stood there silent, wanting to say that I was responsible too, but I just couldn't and didn't. After the whole affair, I realized I was treated differently simply because

I was the leader of the youth organization. Something, in some twisted way, was sorely wrong.

* * * *

Ludwig came back to the table and sat himself down. My bladder was full. Ludwig was sweating from all the dancing. I told him we should leave for the evening as we had a big day ahead of us tomorrow. With some protestation from the others, and from Ludwig, we finally came to a consensus. We excused ourselves from the celebration to get some rest at my grandparent's place.

16hrs00mins: Crossing the Danube

August 19, 1979, 2:00 a.m.: They all waved as we departed. The music was still as loud as ever. The northern breeze had grown into a wind. It helped further along the music in our direction. I had no intention of going to the grandparents at this time. We continued my deception, taking the dirt path to the right toward my grandparents place. We whispered. I wondered whether there was anyone in sight who might still see us. Twenty-five meters away, I peered ahead, behind, and to the side. No one was there. I convinced myself that we were alone. I turned hard left from the path. I yanked Ludwig's arm in my direction. We brushed passed a couple of bushes. They swept back as we passed. We climbed over a small wooden fence. We ran through a very small open corn patch. Beyond the cornhusks, we carried on trampling over a few small gardens. The houses to our left were dark. They held little life in them. We stopped behind a small oak tree on the laneway to the main road. There was no one to our left or right. I estimated we were maybe one hundred meters north of the checkpoint. There were four small houses between us and the guard shack. The breeze was steady and firm coming from that direction.

We could still hear the grumblings of the community center. No one stirred in the house just to our right. Only a few light posts were lit. Neither Ludwig nor I could see any movements by the military in the shack. There wasn't even the light of a burning cigarette. This was the time. We slinked quickly but quietly across the dusty dirt road. We jumped up onto and over a small stone fence and tiptoed across the old railroad. Finally, we slid down the slope about one meter to the bank of the Danube. Everything was black now. We kneeled behind several bushy trees. The bushes concealed us to our left; the railway rose behind us. We couldn't see the road behind us or the guard shack to our left. The Danube was open right in front of us. A chill came over. Goose bumps ran up my arm as I thought of my mother, floating there, chained to a tree.

We stayed low, hidden behind those small bushes. I whispered to Ludwig, imploring him to remove his clothes quickly but quietly. We had to prepare for the swim ahead. From a crouched position, I spilled the contents of the satchel onto the ground. I grabbed one of the plastic bags. There was one bag for Ludwig as well. Two strings fell from the satchel as well. I grabbed one and handed the other to Ludwig.

Silently, we slipped off our shoes and pulled off our socks and pants. We forced them into the plastic bags. I unbuttoned my jacket and in a single motion pulled the jacket and my shirt off. Into the bag they went. We wrapped the mouth of the bags with our strings. We tied the string tightly around our left forearms.

The cold mud and grass squished under our bare feet as we made our last footprints on Romanian soil. The water was cool. And I could smell the black ooze just as I had done before while fishing with Dad. The bottom did not fall away very quickly. It was quite shallow for twenty meters. We tried not to splash but hurried to the deeper water. Grass from the bottom brushed up against our legs and thighs as we slinked ever deeper until finally we were swimming.

"Ludwig, swim quickly. Do the breaststroke, but don't dare to make a noise," I cautioned him. The water was choppy from the wind, and we didn't really notice the current pulling us downstream. I remembered now, as we swam, the ground below us, once planted with corn, and some willow trees, had been flooded after they damned the river at Portile de Fier.

The river had forced us downriver toward the guard shack. We couldn't have been more than one hundred meters away. I still could not distinguish a guard in the shack. Branches scratched against my stomach and feet. It was as though fingers were reaching out to capture me. Again and again, they grazed across me. I shuddered. Was it a snake, or did I imagine capture?

* * * *

At UM 01256, during the second half of my term as a corporal, I was able to leave the camp and go to town every few days. I noticed a young girl on Strada Infratirii on one of my trips. Then I saw her a second time. I acknowledged her but never approached. Later came a third and a fourth encounter. Finally, I approached her. I introduced myself. We chatted for a while. She was a very friendly girl and loved to talk. But I had to take my leave to go back to the base. I arranged with her to meet her later that evening.

Prior to everyone going to bed, I put on my street clothes. I had a sweater from home and a pair of runners. I knew from my guard days the most vulnerable part of the perimeter, so I walked over to it. When I felt it was safe, I jumped the fence.

She was there waiting as we had planned. I felt a little uncomfortable going to her house. I didn't know her parents. I didn't know how they would react. So it was easier just to sit on a park bench. There, we talked for several hours. We told one another stories and flirted.

I was preoccupied with our conversation and missed the approach of a man. For some strange reason, I think I was preconditioned. I missed his approach. But in a split second, as he walked by, I recognized him as an officer. I leapt to my feet and saluted him. The officer was startled. He reared back.

He did not expect anything of the kind. At first, he did not recognize me. I was dressed in street clothes.

"Who the hell are you?" he demanded. I responded. He looked at me dumbfounded. "What the hell are you doing in the city at this time?"

I motioned in the direction of the girl.

He shook his head and escorted me back to the camp. The silence was sobering. This time, I was in real trouble. After a scolding from the commander, I was put into cleaning detail.

* * * *

Swimming along, Ludwig slightly behind at my right side, all was very dark. The clouds from earlier in the day lingered high overhead, hiding the moon and stars. It was an excellent night for concealment. Not even the Danube shimmered from its murky depths. But the wind played against us, pushing waves contrary to our direction. Then I felt it. The rivers' current caught us. It pushed us strongly downstream.

"OK, Ludwig. Swim for your life. Keep up with me, and we can make it!" I implored.

Without a word, we swam on and on and on, focusing on the blackness of the hill on the other side. The monotony of the whole thing gripped at my mind. I concentrated on the stroke of my arms and the kicking of my feet. Forward. Distracted for a moment, I discerned the faint ringing of an alarm. Then it was gone. Had I imagined the noise? Up on the hillside, I could see a faint light coming from Saul's home. We were on our way. Bazias was behind us, and we had slipped away from Romania.

17hrs00mins: The Danube Fights Back

I turned my head to break the monotony of stroke after stroke. Ludwig should be behind me and a little to my left.

I guess time passed by. When I turned to see Ludwig, he was gone. Treading water, the Danube pushed me further downstream as I scanned the water's horizon for Ludwig. Where in the hell could he be? I called out lightly once, hoping to hear his reply. I waited, listening intently. Nothing came in return.

* * * *

One soldier shot himself. He was cleaning his gun and playing with it. He must have accidentally depressed the trigger. The automatic AK-47 shredded a huge wound in his belly. Blood was splattered everywhere. It was on the ceiling and on his bed, and it pooled on the floor. The EMS was called. They used towels and every dressing they had to stop the bleeding. They left a mess behind when they left. Everything was blood soaked and needed to be thrown away. The poor soldiers that cleaned the floors dry heaved as thcy attended to the work. Fortunately, he survived.

* * * *

I kicked and treaded violently as I forced my head out of the water as far as I could. Waves were still in the way. Then again, in near desperation, I risked it all by calling out loudly. The cloud cover, earlier our friend, had become our foe. It was so black; the water was black. The moon was absent. There were no reflections of light upon the Danube. I could not see him.

Fear flooded my thoughts. I started to hyperventilate. Panic engulfed me. I could barely catch a full breath. Finally, a faint shadow emerged barely above the water some twenty-five meters behind. I swam toward the shadow. It was Ludwig. What had transpired? I must have lost track of time. I waited, treading water. He drew near more slowly than I estimated. He made a stroke with his right arm. His left flailed just above the surface. His plastic bag pulled it down.

Ludwig

"Augh!" Gasping for air and choking on the Danube's water . . . OK stay afloat. Just relax. Oh my god, here comes another big wave. I stretched my neck out, kicked against the water, and turned my head away from the white cap. I never imagined it would be this difficult. Where is Doru? Where did he go? I can't see him ahead of me anymore. Why didn't he slow down? Why did he leave me? Oh my god, I'm going to die.

"Augh!" Another wave hit me right in my mouth. Come on, Ludwig; pay attention to what you are doing. OK then. This fucking bag is pulling me down. It's a goddamned anchor now, not a floater. Lactic acid built up in my arms. My arms were heavy, and my shoulder joints were on fire. I fought with the bag. I was losing. I can't see any hole in it. Where is the water coming in? I pulled it closer to my face. I tried to empty the water and tie up any hole that was letting the water in. Oh, it's so damned dark. I can't see, shit!

Where in the hell is Doru? Oh, I want to cry out for help. But what if someone hears me? We're both done for then! There isn't anything moving ahead, but the darkness of the far side was blackening. I've got to make it!

What was that? Did I hear something? OK, I quieted my arms as long as I could and listened intently toward the black of the far bank. My arms are so tired. I am so cold. I can just feel my fingers, and the damn bag is cutting into my wrist. Shit. I'm going to cut it off before it becomes the end of me and pulls me to the bottom.

Hey, I'm sure I heard something. It sounded like my name coming from ahead and to the left. I scanned the water ahead. There. I think I see something. Is it Doru's head? It has to be! He was waving his hand now. I shouted back, waving my free right hand as much as I dared and simply could manage. The damn bag pulled me down, and the waves kept hitting me square in the face. How has Doru managed? "OK, Ludwig," I talked to myself, "swim toward Doru, but don't let him get out of your sight."

I stroked with my right hand and pulled the bag with my left. I kicked with what little energy remained, strengthened now only by adrenaline, I am sure. Why is he moving away? He is getting further away. "Wait up!" I shouted. "Wait up! Wait for me!" Doru's head was still there. So again and again, I crawled and dragged my way toward him. Oh, I was finally making some ground. Doru was waiting there, treading in the water.

Finally, I could see his face. It felt so good; I was so tired and scared.

* * * *

"What in the hell are you doing? You scared the shit out of me! Keep up to my side, man." Ludwig looked scared as I scolded him.

"Doru, I am fucked," he gasped.

"Why, what is wrong?" I pleaded.

"My fucking bag is full of water. It is so heavy. I can barely swim anymore," he said. "I am exhausted." A larger wave struck him face on. Ludwig gasped, spitting out the water, searching for air. "I don't think I am going to make it, Doru! If I can't, just save yourself."

One hour out, basically in the middle of the Danube, my bag floated well. Here, the water was deep. We were right in the middle of the channel, and the current ran briskly. *What to do now?* I asked myself. "OK, Ludwig, what kind of bullshit talk is this? You are scaring the hell out of me! *Together, either we are both going to make it or neither of us will!*" I assured him. Jesuus Christ. The thought scared me to death. At the same time, I am sure a rush of adrenaline gave me strength of resolve. I couldn't fail. We just had to make it!

"Ludwig, take hold of my bag, and help me to swim," I told him. And he did.

Together again, we nudged into one another. Fear overcame me out in the middle of this damn river. Up until now, we had had the good fortune of not coming into contact with any Romanian patrol boats. Nor had we been taken down by rogue drifting logs. But Yugoslavia was still a long dream away. My mind raced now, remembering our conversation with Captain Stefan. Would we too drown in the river, dragged down by debris? Or would a passing boat run us down? Or even worse, would the patrols catch us and gun us down into a watery grave? I remembered those huge catfish the fishermen would bring to shore. What if one of those got ahold of me?

* * * *

After the first forty-five days of military training, I had to take an oath to be loyal to Romania. I had to fight to the end to be free!

* * * *

Ludwig struggled. At times, he grabbed on to me with both of his hands. I felt I was going down as well. He was just above water. I stopped swimming for a moment to reassure Ludwig that we were getting nearer to our destination. Again, he swallowed a mouthful of that putrid Danube water.

"Ludwig, turn your head away from the wind so that the wind hits the back of your head," I scolded him. He had never swum in such a large river like I did as a kid. His fatigue worsened with each gasping breath of air. Trying this new method helped a little. He got clear, deeper breaths of air. It seemed to give him a little more courage. He let go with one hand. We went a little faster now as I helped him swim.

My foot grazed something. Was it that rogue log? I looked up for a quick moment. I could distinguish trees more clearly now. The bank's edge was not far away. Ludwig stopped stroking and looked up too. We almost relaxed a moment as the current seemed to relax as well. My toes scratched just barely at the bottom. Energized, we pushed forward until we were swimming and walking in nearly equal portions.

Pain shot through my leg! Sand and mud oozed around my foot and ankle. I could feel a burning sensation in my legs all the way to my groin. What was happening? Again panic flooded my emotions. *OK, calm yourself, Doru,* I told myself. A sudden realization came over me just how cold my core had become from the water and the fear. I was close to hypothermia. I could only image how Ludwig must feel.

Excited, we pulled one another and our water-logged plastic bags to shore. We fell on the sandy, muddy beach. We were exhausted. But we had made it!

We looked back across to Romania. It was dark, very, very dark. We could see the outline of the mountains against the gray of the sky. We had fought against the Danube's great breadth and power, and we had won. Barely! We must have been crazy to attempt such a feat.

Chugga, chugga. A motor not too far away labored along. Then upstream, out from the darkness, the outline of a tugboat revealed itself. Large and now frightfully menacing, it pulled five very long barges behind it. Its speed was ominous, combined with the flow of the Danube. Whatever relief I felt now away from Romania was swept away by panic as I imagined entering the Danube half an hour later. The success we enjoyed now certainly would have become tragic disaster.

18hrs00mins: Yugoslavia: Wet Pants

August 19, 1979, 4:00 a.m.: We sat on the same bank, where as a kid, I saw farmers grazing their cattle. We collected our thoughts and caught our breath. The cool breeze quickly chilled us. A dim light on the far side bounced moving downstream. I conjectured the light was that of the miner's transport as it rounded the corner from Socol onto the Danube. That placed us about three kilometers downstream, at about four o'clock in the morning, two hours after we began our swim.

We gathered our plastic bags and went further up the bank to get dressed. Ludwig's clothes were soaked. We hadn't taken enough time to check the bags for holes. It didn't matter now anyway. Ludwig wrung his clothes out as best he could. He slapped them against a nearby tree. Mine were wet too as I poured them and then water onto the grass. Water must have crept in past the knot in the mouth of the bag.

Quickly, we dressed. It was very uncomfortable. The clothes had a rotten stench to them as well. We had to go west as far away from the Danube as we could get from Romania. The wet pants against our already damp skin gave us no comfort and little extra warmth. We didn't want to be caught by Serbian soldiers this close to the border. This close to the border, maybe they'd just send us back or put us in jail for illegally crossing the border. In any event, stories from the elder folk in my village of a road that went to the Serbian village of Ram and then onward to Belgrade came to mind. That's what we needed to find next. And then find transport.

Tall corn and grains grew in the fields that we rambled across. Little heads of the grains dislodged and planted themselves on our clothes. It was still very dark. Clouds still covered the night sky. It hid any stars that might be there. No one nor animal could be seen nor heard. Eerie. But we continued on in search of that road. Two hundred meters through several gardens, we found the edge of the road. Not knowing where exactly we were, we decided to turn right and walk to the nearest village, whatever or wherever that might be.

We laughed a little and sang out loud, now releasing all the pent-up stress. We had made it!

"Man was I scared when you said you couldn't make it!" I joked.

More seriously, Ludwig thanked me, "You saved my life. Really! I know I would have been finished without you." The practice back in Reşiţa must have paid off. "Phew!"

Almost trotting down the road, we quickly covered several kilometers. We skipped, almost dancing with the excitement of freedom ahead of us. Then from the rear came headlights. As the vehicle neared, I questioned what to do. Could it be border patrol? Should we get off the road now and hide or wave it down and ask for a ride? Ludwig and I stood to the side and waved downward trying to get its attention to stop. A Mercedes, it had a German license plate. Immediately, I told Ludwig to keep quiet for a while. I told him to let me speak in Serbian to gain their trust. He could try speaking German later.

The car stopped, and the passenger rolled down his window. The driver got out of the car and came around the front to see us.

"Hey, there, can you give us a ride to the next village?" I inquired in Serbian.

The passenger retorted, "What in the *hell* are you guys doing out here? Got nothing better to do than wander the streets at night?" He got out of the vehicle. "We've got five already so why not a couple more. Hop in!" Ludwig got in the back while I sat in the front between passenger and the driver.

All was quiet for a bit. They discussed something among themselves of which I tried to pay some attention. "Stop!" called out one passenger.

"Why?" The driver looked across.

"*Stop* the fucking car! Now! Damn it!" he yelled.

Oh my god, now what? I straightened back into the seat as I turned my eyes toward him. I leaned my body back away from his. He put his hand on my left thigh.

"Why in the hell are you so wet? I know it has been raining but not so much as to drench you. Where are you guys from anyway?" he demanded.

Thinking for but a moment, I said, "We are from Ram."

Immediately, he jerked his head back; his eyes rose to my face, in an inquisitive manner, then down, measuring the rest of me. "Bullshit, motherfucker!" he yelled. "I am from Ram, and I've never seen you before. Don't bullshit me!" He cursed.

Now I was really scared. I wanted to tell him the truth earlier, but the words just wouldn't come out of my mouth. I stammered, "OK, OK." I shook my hands in the air in front of me. "We just swam across the Danube."

"Come on. Are you serious?" he questioned me.

By this time, Ludwig too was standing on the road beside the car, perplexed, not understanding the Serbian conversation. "Ya, really. Our clothes are still wet from the swim. We just escaped from Romania," I explained.

"No way. You guys must be crazy! It's like two kilometers across." He looked at the others in bewilderment. He laughed uneasily. I actually think we swam closer to four kilometers as the Danube pushed us downriver to where the Danube turns directly to the east.

"We could really use a break now. If you guys could help us out, we would really appreciate it . . . But if you can't, then so be it," I conceded.

They all shook their heads, in amazement, I guess, and motioned for us to get back into the car. The passenger slapped my thigh hard again as he sat back down and closed the door. We were on our way again.

Our conversation switched from Serbian to German and back again. We all smoked their cigarettes. They remained fixated with the crossing of the Danube for some time before they asked us where we were going.

"We hope to get to the Austrian border. We heard there is a refugee camp there," I explained our plan to them.

"Huh. How are you getting there?" Again, the passenger asked.

"I'm not really sure. Probably just hitch rides there," I said.

"Man, you'll get caught that way for sure. You guys should take the train," he added.

"Maybe so, but we don't have any money for that," I explained.

Bemused, he commented, "You guys really are crazy. How in the hell do you think you are going to go all that way with no money?" He paused a moment. "And what were you planning on eating?" Shaking his head in disbelief, he told me they would help us out. They gathered some money between them all and gave it to me. "OK, here is enough money to get you a bus ticket to Belgrade. After that you are on your own. Good luck!"

They stopped the car at the bus station in Kličevac. We shook hands and thanked him for their help. The passenger noticed that I wasn't wearing any socks. "Where are your socks?" He asked, shaking his head again in disbelief.

I had forgotten about them in the car ride. "Oh, I lost them on the shore of the Danube when I dumped my clothes out of the plastic bag," I told him.

He must have really felt sorry for us because he sat back into the seat, took his shoes then his socks off, and gave them to me to wear. "Keep yourselves warm, guys, and good luck." They sped off on their journey to Germany. They were some good guys. I felt bad about lying to them about not having any money. I wasn't sure though if the money we had would allow us to get to the border.

Our timing couldn't have been better. Fifteen minutes later, the bus arrived en route to Belgrade. No one, except for the lady behind the ticket booth, was awake this early in the morning. Only a very few passengers occupied the seats. They didn't even look up at us as we made our way to a seat. They were all asleep. The lady at the ticket booth said it would take us three hours to get to Belgrade.

Our enthusiasm of freedom turned to utter exhaustion as we sat staring out into the darkness of the very early morning. My eyes must have closed because when they opened next, it was to the pain of the sun rising. Buildings surrounded our bus. Ludwig was still asleep, so I nudged him. We had come all the way to Belgrade.

24hrs00mins: Belgrade: Rid of the Mud

August 19, 1979, 10:00 a.m.: I rubbed the dirt from my eyes. I anticipated our arrival at the bus station. People were all over, bustling and hustling about. I saw what looked to be a fruit market on one street. I was amazed by how much was available. Apples. Ahead of us, lots of buses were going on their way, mostly full. Pears. Ours came to a halt not far from the main building. There was a line of people waiting, apparently to board this bus off to some other destination or maybe returning to the Danube. Corn. I was surprised by just how busy everything seemed to be yet organized.

As we stepped down from the bus and onto the platform, the woman in the front of the line looked strangely at me. Anyway, we walked over to a building. Here, we were out of the way of the crowd. We paused to gather ourselves and make a plan. Ludwig looked at me, and I at him as we stopped. Oh my god, our clothes were absolutely filthy, especially from the knees down. They were damp and soiled with sand and mud, as well as corn and grain pieces picked up along our hike from the Danube to the road. We stood out like peasants who escaped from Romania.

"Excuse me, sir, can you help us?" I asked an elderly gentleman passing by. "Do you know where we could find some clothes for sale?"

"Oh yes. For sure," he remarked. We were dishevelled, and with one glance, he told us that. He pointed around the corner. "You are in luck. There is a market just around the corner."

We thanked him then sped away hiding among the crowd in the market. I could not believe the sights. It was the largest market I had ever seen. There were loads of food, trinkets, fruits, vegetables, carpets, shoes, shirts, and pants. We had the urge to buy the first pair we saw. But there were so many people and so much variety that we ended up just walking and looking in disbelief. We checked prices and sizes. I had three thousand Romanian lei and Ludwig five hundred DM. So we chose carefully and bought socks, underwear, a shirt, and pullover, as well as the denim pants we really needed. Ludwig found a sweater. It was red across the shoulders and dark blue below the chest. A nearby public washroom afforded us a place to clean up and change into our new clothes. My fear dissipated. I felt more confident now. We could pass for Yugoslav youths.

The next train to Austria wasn't for another two and a half hours. My stomach grumbled with hunger. First though, we decided to change some German DM to pay for the train tickets. The dinars we received as change in the market wouldn't quite cover the total. Rather than returning to the market, we happened across a busy wicket for currency exchange. We stood our turn in line. We were used to queuing for everything, for anything, but usually for nothing. We counted our money. We discussed the exchange rate. We calculated how much we needed to change. A finger from behind tapped me on the shoulder. I froze immediately. I was startled by the prospect of capture by the authorities.

"Hey, I'll give you a better rate to change those DM," whispered a man's voice.

Still in shock, I turned casually. I looked at the young man and then at Ludwig as if to ask for his permission. The line was still quite long. "OK, as long as you give us a better rate." Agreed, we exited the line and turned around the corner where we made the deal. He gave us a little more, making it worth our while.

We returned to the main building and went quickly directly to the train sales wicket without a lineup.

"Two tickets to Maribor, please," I commanded the salesman behind the bars.

"Return?" he asked.

"No. We just need one way," I said.

"It's the same price," he added.

"No, I don't know when we'll use them. We are going to work there," I lied.

"You can use them for the next six months," he told me.

"Nah, we won't use them," I said. He gave me a look of disbelief. Then he simply filled my order and took the money.

Two hours before the train would depart, there was plenty of time to get a good meal. We ate a huge feast. As always, we were concerned we wouldn't eat for some time again. With little to do but watch the departure board, we mulled about and pretended to be Yugoslavians waiting to go home.

Our train wasn't full when we left Belgrade. We managed to find an empty compartment for ourselves; however, a few hours out, after we had caught a little sleep, more passengers boarded and helped themselves to the empty space. Most had several bags. I heard that they were on their way to Vienna. Interested, I listened intently but feigned not to look so. Later, I motioned Ludwig to join me in the hallway for a smoke.

"Ludwig, I heard these Serbians talking about going to work in Vienna. Maybe they could give us some help. What do you think?" I asked. Ludwig agreed, so when we got back into the compartment, I joined the conversation. After a short bit, maybe five minutes, one of them asked me where we were from. Upon my tentative answer, silence came over the compartment. One of the passengers closest to the exit closed the door and locked it.

Before the tension built too much, I began to tell our story of how we had just escaped from Romania. I asked them for help if they could in directing us to the Austrian border refugee camp. They were mystified by our story. One of them went out of the compartment and returned with several beers. He was prepared for a long story.

"You'd be better off not going to Austria. The camps there are full of emigrants," one guy said. "I heard there is a lot of bad stuff going on there too. People are pretty desperate," said another. "Why don't you try the Italian border at Trieste instead?" added another. "Yes, it's probably better there. I heard it is not so full. You might even be able to find some better work there too."

I listened intently, translated for Ludwig, and wondered how we could get to Italy.

"How can we get to Italy from here though?" I asked.

"Don't you worry. We'll tell you when to get off this train," they reassured me.

"Oh ya. I remember the best place to get off. Ljubljana, west of Zagreb," commented another Serbian. "Ya, you're right, but do you know what? They should buy tickets from there onward to the stop prior to the border. Otherwise, they'll need to have passports with a visa." "Shit. Ya, I forgot about that. Don't go to the border. That'll raise too many suspicions." "What is the name of that last stop? Can you remember?" "I think it is Sezanna. You'd be better to get off there and walk the rest from there. Hopefully, you can elude the police and make it right into Trieste."

37hrs00mins: Ljubljana:
Stay Out of the Rain

August 19, 1979, 11:00 p.m.: Unlike Belgrade and Zagreb, Ljubljana had a very modest train station. Outside the station, there were plenty of bars nearby to enjoy a beer while we waited for the train. On our way to a nearby bar, a group of drunken soldiers passed us by. They stumbled to and fro, singing, shouting, and arguing. "Death to Tito! Long live, Tito!" I couldn't even imagine such conflicting views being openly shared with anyone who passed.

The bar was a single small room with several small tables scattered about. All barstools were taken. We looked around. I gave Ludwig the Slovenian newspaper I found at the front door and motioned for him to take the empty table toward the center of the room while I went for some drinks.

The bar tender was an old chap who talked freely with everyone. I ordered a couple beers, two coffees, and a pastry to dip. As I waited for the order, policemen entered the bar. The first was clearly in charge. He was followed by a couple of his underlings. They walked up to the bar, near to where I was standing, and the officer announced that he was checking identification documents and to make them ready. Ludwig looked over to me and to the officer but didn't understand the gravity of the situation. As the officer checked the fellow to my left, the barman filled my order, and I paid. With the tray and its contents in hand, I walked past the officer, between two tables, and around another. Carefully, I placed the tray on the table, seated myself, took a piece of the newspaper, and handed another portion to Ludwig. Ludwig looked at me strangely. I knew he couldn't read Slovenian, but neither could I for that matter.

We sat there, hidden behind the newspaper, pretending to read, sipping at our coffee from time to time. I contemplated what to do. It would be too obvious to leave a full order on the table. Surely the guard at the door wouldn't allow us to leave anyway. Well, this was our fate to be captured at a bar in Ljubljana. I took a big long swallow from my beer stein. I may as well enjoy my beer as it was probably the last I would have for some time. Ludwig, still behind the paper, still had no idea of what was about to happen.

At least ten minutes passed before he finished checking the IDs of everyone on the bar stools. Another five minutes passed as he started at the table in front of us. For certain, we would be checked next. He pointed at the table to the right and checked two of the three IDs. Then, as though bored, the officer backtracked. He turned and walked out of the bar as suddenly as he had entered. Jesuus Christ, our luck. The grace of God must have been looking down upon us. Quietly, in Romanian, I told Ludwig what had just happened.

We clanked our beer glasses indiscreetly at table level, slowly finishing the beer, coffee, and the pastry before exiting the bar as well. The train wasn't scheduled to depart for some time still. We mixed in with what few people there were and acted as though we were one of them.

39hrs00mins: The Sun
Breaks from the Night

August 20, 1979, 01:00 a.m.: From my calculations, the train, a high speed one, was scheduled to arrive in Trieste in about four and a half hours. That meant we needed to get off some time before that.

Ludwig and I sat awake alone on this train. A few travelers slept on the seats behind us. Once we left the lights of the city, all was black. We sat there staring out the black windows. The surrounding hills and trees of the forest made it feel even darker.

We passed the cities of Vrhnika, Logatec, Postojna, and Senožeče. We needed to get off very soon, but should we wait for the last stop or get off one before?

We decided on Divača. There we stood, in the darkness of the very early morning, no idea really of where we were, how far we've come, or what direction to take to go to Trieste. And once there, we really had no idea of how to find this refugee camp. Would it be that obvious?

On both sides of the track, a dense dark forest rose up the hillsides. It seemed logical at the time to just continue on down the tracks, this time walking though. So off we went, kicking stones and hopping from tie to tie. The darkness increased as we moved away from the train stop and around a mountain.

Fortunately, the tracks shone brightly by the light of the moon on this clear evening. The stars were bright too as we pointed out constellations to one another.

We walked and walked and talked, about nothing of interest really, as the time passed by hour by hour and the distance kilometer by kilometer. How much farther could it possibly be? Would the morning sun break sometime soon?

The track rumbled; a noise so loud and apparently so very close to us rang out. But where was it coming from, ahead or behind? It was a train concealed by the mountain turns, that was certain. Ludwig and I prepared for an escape. Both sides of tracks sloped steeply downward into the dark of the forest. Where could we go?

Ahead of us now, the lights of the train nearly blinded us. Oh my god, it was one of those fast ones coming at full speed. I jumped down the slope to the right and Ludwig to the left. It was deafening as it passed, causing the earth to tremble and those small rocks to leap from beside the rails, scattering about the slope.

"Jesuus Christ!" I yelled. "That was too close."

"Holy shit! That was unbelievable!" Ludwig yelled, pulled himself back to the tracks, and jumped about. Our eyes were wide open now, and our senses screamed out, heightened by an unanticipated fear. We continued on at an increased gallop, hindered only by the unevenness of the ties and the stones.

Out in the distance, through branches of the trees, we could see a dim light. Deciding that it must be a roadside lamp, we started in its direction. Down the railroad track shoulder, we jumped from heel to heel, zigging and zagging like a skier making his way to the bottom of the slope. Once at the bottom, we backsighted the tracks to establish our course of direction through the forest ahead. Fortunately, the forest turned quickly into a grainfield. The opening allowed us to see the direction of the road ahead.

The sun rose over the mountains behind us as we walked down the road. Few cars passed us at first. The flow of traffic steadily increased as we hiked on for the next half hour. I calculated that it must be around 6:00 a.m. A convoy of green, tarp-covered trucks passed us. They were military style. We figured that we must be getting close to the border now.

From around a sharp corner, a large wide truck quickly approached. We veered further onto the gravel shoulder. It felt a little safer distance to allow the vehicles to pass in both directions. As the truck bore down on us though, we questioned the safety of our distance. Its breaks squealed as the truck pulled onto the gravel right in front of us. We reared up, prepared to leap at the last moment. The truck came to a halt. As the truck rocked to a standstill, out jumped the driver. He jumped out onto the pavement. A cloud of dust shot up from the release of air from the brakes.

He came directly toward us and put a smoke to his lips. "Got a light?" he asked.

Startled, "Ya, sure we do." I pulled what was left of a matchbook from my pocket. I lit his cigarette. He offered us one, and we had a smoke too. The driver told us about how his truck lighter was busted and how had meant to fix it, etc. etc. Then as quickly as he stopped, he clambered back into his truck. Before he closed the door, I inquired, "How far is it to Sežana?"

"Just a few hundred meters around the bend," he remarked. His truck roared off of the shoulder.

We had almost walked straight into the border crossing. Any further and we surely would have been caught before we had the chance to look for the refugee camp. As we walked on another fifty meters, we discussed what to do. We decided to go into the bush and make our way from there. Hopefully, we would go unnoticed around the border crossing and on then on to find the camp. The forest was dense and much darker than back on the road. The route was uneven; I feared that we might not even be going in the right direction. However, we should come to some sort of border demarcation soon. Then we'd know if we were in Italy.

Those few hundred meters turned into kilometers. I doubted the directions from the truck driver; I doubted our decision to turn from the road. We came across paths in the forest. I imagined they were worn in by soldiers on border patrols. Maybe we'll get caught; maybe we should get caught? We're so close now, they wouldn't turn us back. But we carried on through the trees and found ourselves climbing over rocks piled neatly as fences. Every hundred meters, we climbed another fence and then another. I had not anticipated this sort of torture.

The sun was full now, and the morning was getting very hot. We had no water, and we were sweating from overexertion. That beer in Ljubljana came to mind more than once. It was still my last for some time. Finally, at a high point, dejected and almost beaten, we came to a clearing and could see for some ways across a valley and over to the mountains ahead. There was a good cleared line ahead that stretched straight through the forest, across the valleys, and over the hills. *Could it be the Italian border?* I wondered. So we continued on to it.

The line had been cleared for a power line. The poles held many large wires. We surmised that it must be an important one leading to a large town. From pole to pole, we walked, more easily than in the forest, at a good pace but not too fast. We were hungry and hot. But we were really thirsty. At least we were going in a determined direction without the fear of walking in circles. Where this would take us was the only question.

From another high point, we could see far ahead enough to see a town. There was also another cut line perpendicular to ours some two or three kilometers before the town. My mind raced. Could that be the border? I questioned why we did not see any sort of border guards or towers or a fence at least. In any event, we were going to find out. We kept to the side of the cut line, concealed a little by trees. On we went for a while; distances over the mountains were greater than it appeared.

As we neared this new cut line, I noticed that the signs were in Serbian, warning of danger. And when we crossed over that line, the first sign had changed. Could it be? Had we crossed the border? No one was there to even care? Ludwig was skeptical and ran up to the next post. That sign too was in Italian. OK, we must have done it! But we needed to look at one more over the next little rise. It was the same. Surely we had come all the way to Italy. We embraced one another tightly. Yes, we had really escaped to the west!

50hrs00mins: Gropada: Escape the Reign

August 20, 1979, 11:00 a.m.: A town, which I later learned to be Gropada, was in clear view now, down and off to the left through the forest. Further on, in line with the cut line, there stood a huge building. It was all by itself. Somehow drawn to it, I wondered what such a large building could possibly be used for.

The village had more pull though. I was so hungry and thirsty. I called out in Serbian to a small group of goat herders. They acknowledged us. They acted as though they didn't quite understand. I had the distinct impression they were just staying away from us. Oh well, I thought they must be Italians. Anyway, we saw a small bistro sign in the town. We hiked out of the forest, across some fields, and onto the narrow streets of the village. Nothing but food was on my mind.

It was a quaint place made of stone. It was near empty. Only one young couple sat at a table. The deli bar smelled of beer and wine, smattered with the aroma of the prosciutto ham that hung from the ceiling. Oh, we were in heaven. In Serbian, I ordered two great big mugs of beer, two packs of Marlboros, and sandwiches to eat.

"Panini?" the barman asked. I nodded.

Whatever panini was, it sounded Italian, and it sounded great. It turned out even better than that. He piled a mountain of prosciutto and cheese on freshly baked bread. Oh, I could only just wait to eat it.

As he passed me the plate, I told him we had only Serbian money to pay. Not taken aback in the least, he said, "Whatever money you have, it is all good here!"

Ludwig smiled with happiness. A feast was ahead of us. We sat, chewed on the sandwich, and washed it down with the beer. Our conversation ceased as we concentrated at the purpose at hand. Behind us, the couple talked. They were quiet. The spoke in a language I couldn't place. That sandwich was so good. I was full and content. Any fear we had that had built up over the past two days was pushed aside by the fullness!

I wondered if the couple were immigrants or possibly refugees. Ludwig noticed them too and suggested we follow them for a short while to see where they might lead us. They must have been here for some time as they weaved their way through the narrow streets surrounded by stone houses. Then they took a foot path through a treed area with smaller garden plots on either side. Eventually, we came to a larger path for horse carts. From there, we could see a major highway. We saw them dash across and then out of sight. We followed them as quickly as we dared. I suppose we were one hundred meters behind but took us a while to cross the busy highway. Luckily, there was a path on the far side, or we would have lost them completely.

Through yet another small treed area, we came out into a clearing. That now familiar massive building was directly in front of us. A large fence built of half inch square steel, fifty meters and a small guard shack stood between us. The young couple stopped there. They were talking to someone. Curious, we followed them to the shack. A woman within asked in Italian for my ID card.

"Ce dracu, pizda masi e aici?"

"What the hell was this?" I muttered in Romanian.

Recognizing my language, the couple turned and asked, "Are you Romanian?" Surprised, I now knew they had been speaking in Romanian at the bistro.

"Ba da." Yes, we are. I answered in Romanian.

"De unde a-ti venit?" They asked us where we were coming from.

"De la Romania." I told them from Romania.

Baffled, they said, "Nu te cred!" They didn't believe our bullshit. I assured them it was so and that we were looking for the refugee camp in Trieste. Amazed, they called a few police guards over to us.

"Don't worry. Come with us. You are here! Go with them. They'll take you inside and ask a few questions. They need to know your name and where you are from."

I couldn't believe our luck. We had actually walked straight to where we wanted to be. We didn't even know it.

51hrs00mins: Trieste: Italian Refugee Camp

August 20, 1979, 11:30 a.m.: We followed another male officer from the guard shack across the courtyard maybe fifty meters. The building was a massive gray cement block structure. Two men caught my attention as they waved at us from behind a wall of stone. I immediately recognized them from my factory in Reşiţa. I waved in return and shouted to them that we would meet after my processing. It was all so exciting yet stressful, not knowing the process ahead of me. Through two small doors, away from the larger main entrance, we entered the building. Inside, another man escorted us to a locked room and left us there for some time.

The room was sparse with four wooden chairs around an oval table. It was bright with fluorescent lighting from above. A gentleman in a suit greeted us and gestured to us to sit. A few moments later, two others joined us in the room. A translator greeted us in Romanian. The other carried files full of forms. He placed them on the table before us.

The translator began, first asking our names, then that of our parents, onto our mother's maiden names, our age, weight, eye and hair color, and then to where we lived, where we worked, and what we did there. It was all very formal and to the point. They filled out the forms with the information we provided them. At some point, another gentleman entered the room with a camera. We stood, one at a time, in front of a simple backdrop on the wall. He left immediately thereafter. I added at every opportunity to tell them that I had left my wife and son behind and wanted to send for them.

Then the interrogation began. The one who spoke Romanian asked us when we had left. "We left Romania at about 2:00 a.m. on the nineteenth," I responded.

"That's only fifty-one hours ago! That's impossible!" he said somewhat agitatedly then translated for the officers. Conferring with them, "Now really, tell me the truth. You are safe here now."

"No really!" I quipped. "We swam across the Danube, hidden by the darkness of the night." I reached into my pocket. "We were lucky to get a ride to the bus station. They were kind enough to give us some money, and one even gave me his pair of socks as I had lost mine on the shore. We got on the bus directly thereafter that took us all the way to Belgrade where we caught a train for Austria."

The officer interrupted me. "So how did you get here?"

I pulled my identification booklet out of my pants. "You see, our compartment filled up with Serbians at one of the stops. I speak Serbian, and Ludwig speaks German. They told us the camps in Austria were overfull, and lots of bad things were going on. They suggested we come here." I placed my identification booklet on the table in front of the translator.

"And no one caught you two coming all this way? You surely must have come from the police authorities." He reached across and picked up my booklet. He looked up at me as his fingers touched the booklet. "This booklet is wet," he remarked.

"Sir, I am telling you the truth. It must still be wet from our swim in the Danube. You see, water leaked into our plastic bags, and we had to buy some new clothes at the market in Belgrade."

Another man entered the room with more papers and a small steel inkpad. Ludwig went first, pushing his pinky finger into the inkblot and then onto the squares indicated on the paper. He started with his right hand and then with his left. All the while, the translator flicked through the pages past my picture and past my red stamp. The booklet was still quite damp and stuck to his fingers. "OK then. This is quite amazing."

I gave my fingerprints once Ludwig was done. Finally, he asked where we would like to emigrate to.

Ludwig spoke up, "I have relatives in Germany. We are planning to go be with them."

Two of the officers got up and left, apparently satisfied with our story, leaving the translator behind. "OK. You guys are all processed now. I'll take you over to the supplies store. Then you might as well go and get a shower before lunch."

The storeroom had everything you need to keep clean. We picked a razor and some extra blades, some shaving cream, a towel, soap, and shampoo. I was puzzled by what I had heard about refugee camps. With our arms and hands full, the officer led us over to our sleeping quarters. Several Albanians rested on their beds in a quite large room of twenty beds or so. They pointed out two empty ones side by side that we put our stuff down on. Again, the officer asked if there was anything else we required before taking his leave.

We lied down only briefly, testing their softness before going off toward the shower rooms. The officer said lunch would be served in another thirty minutes; so we had time to clean up, relax, and then see for ourselves what else the refugee camp had in store. The quickest way to the showers was through the courtyard outside, so we took it. There were lots of people gathering around now. I heard someone speaking Bulgarian, another speaking Hungarian, and several others in Romanian. As we approached them, I was astonished to find that one of the men was from our workplace in Reşiţa. He had escaped with his young son. Mia's husband, Stefan, was there too. We hugged for a time. We were grateful to be safe.

The crowd of refugees had grown substantially since, and everyone stood in line, waiting their turn to get lunch. It was all quite civilized though compared to the mayhem we endured in the food lines back home. No one pushed, shoved, or yelled.

I heard lots of conversations in all sorts of languages. Neither ethnicity nor citizenship meant little here. Toward the front, we picked up a tray, plastic utensils, and napkins. Behind the counter, several women in fishnet hair served the food. We began with soup and a main course of meat, potatoes, and vegetables and finished with fresh fruits.

Ludwig and I made our way to a table where our Romanian friends had saved us chairs. On the way, I questioned the reality of our situation. The living quarters were clean, not overcrowded. We had just had a great hot shower, and the food looked great. We shook hands and kissed cheeks as Romanians do. We were introduced to others at the table before sitting at our places. I really wasn't all that hungry after having just eaten that huge Panini. However, as we shared our adventures, it was apparent that the food was very good.

"Have you seen my wife in the past little while?" one man asked.

"Yes, I have," I said. "In fact, Ofelia and I just saw her the day before Ludwig and I crossed the Danube. She looks fine." She didn't say very much, and what she did was very reserved. At the time, I had not even considered that their son was also absent for a reason. "How did you two get here?" I asked.

"We came across the Danube too. I used an inner tube as a float for me and my boy," he explained. "We were lucky not to come across anything out there, but we got caught by the police on our way across Yugoslavia. We were there for a couple of weeks before they sent us here."

"What was that like?" I asked.

"It was really OK, really. They kept us out of the general criminal population, I think, because my son was with me. Others though were sent to prison until their identities could be confirmed," he said. "It was really strange though how we finally got here. One night, they put ten of us in the back of a police van. They didn't tell us anything. They shut the doors and drove off for several hours. I had no idea of where we going until the van finally stopped. They opened the doors. The policemen told us to get off. He pointed us in the direction of the building we are now in."

At lunch's end, I just had to ask if the food was always like this.

With little else to do, we decided to retire to our beds. I thought it was funny how I didn't realize how tired I had become. Everything was new and unknown. That bed felt so comfortable. I fell quickly to sleep. The stress left my body. We had really made it!

Four hours later . . . I awoke to an incredible noise. It wasn't like a sudden thud or a massive crash. It was a constant roar that was getting louder and louder and closer. Ludwig stirred as well. More and more, it sounded like it was coming from outside our window. What could it be? Our curiosity mixed with a sense of fear forced us to the window. What was in front of our eyes I had never before imagined. The courtyard was packed with people—Asian people. Where could they all have come from? Others already at the refugee camp had brought them out into the courtyard. They met them from every door. Ludwig told me he had never seen an Asian other than on television before. I suppose most of the other refugees never had either.

The clock on the wall read near 5:00 p.m. We had slept more than I realized. It was almost dinnertime. I wondered how they would feed so many people, us included. I worried about this for some time. I am not sure why. I didn't feel hungry. Maybe things would really change for the worse now, like in Austria. Oh, that would not be good.

As we stared from our window, I noticed several cars and vans approaching the compound. Once they stopped in a clearer view, I could tell they were newspeople with cameras, video cameras, and audiotapes. This was more of an event than I had already appreciated. Amazingly too, more and more reporters arrived to report the story. There was quite a commotion, but surprisingly, the Asians were processed quickly and sent to another wing of the huge building.

The reporters stayed and made their way to the cafeteria. It was dinnertime now; and Ludwig and I decided to venture there to get a better view of our new friends and, of course, to make sure we got our share of food. To our disbelief, many of the others had had the same idea as well. They formed an orderly food line, just like at dinner. As we waited our turn, the reporters interviewed several of the refugees as they ate their meals. It was some time before the Asians entered the dining hall.

It looked to me that whole families had come. I saw one family that included elderly grandparents to tiny newly born babies. The reporters were certainly interested in them and took a profusion of videos and photos. The family must have been overwhelmed by all the attention. But they stood in line and waited their turn.

I was even more amazed than earlier at lunch. All utensils were brand-new silverware. No more plastic. And there was even a greater selection of food. As well as soup and the main course, there were fruits and sweets. The facility must have been forewarned of the new refugees and all the media attention they would garner. At the end of the meal, we went our way, and they went theirs.

End of Day One

For the next couple of days, Ludwig and I were kept in quarantine. It was a different kind of quarantine than I originally thought it would be. All it meant was we had to stay in the building while they confirmed our identities and gave us a refugee identity card. After that, we were allowed to leave the building. We weren't encouraged to find work, but they made it clear that we would need some money to pay for extra personal things during our stay. The news of newcomers spread quickly throughout the camp. The Albanians knew when new Albanians refugees arrived, the Bulgarians knew when new Bulgarians arrived, and we were no different. It seemed amazing how someone always knew someone else who knew the new arrivals. We all came from such a small world.

One morning an American Romanian and his girlfriend arrived at the camp. He had brought her from Serbia after she had used her passport privilege to escape. She was one of the lucky ones. She was a communist party member, who had been given a passport to conduct small import business back into Romania. Ludwig and I joined the small group and found ourselves talking about the refugee camp. The man was planning on returning to Romania the next day to visit his family. Listening intently to his plans, I thought it possible that he could deliver a letter for me to Ofelia. So out of the blue, I simply asked him. He had no troubles with it and told me to make sure I gave it to him before he left that evening.

Somehow I felt skeptical whether he would indeed be bothered to post the letter. He even refused the funds to pay for a stamp. I figured there would be nothing lost anyway and went about writing a four-page letter. In it, I told Ofelia that I was OK and in the refugee camp here in Trieste. I missed her and Liviu already, but it was my last best chance to escape. With absolute certainty, I assured her that the three of us would be together again and that I would do all I could to make that time as short as possible. In the end, I wrote that I would call her shortly. The envelope was left without a return address so as not to alert anyone who may be inquiring of my whereabouts. I thought it safer for Ofelia. The man took my letter and left behind his girlfriend to go through the system just as we were doing.

Ofelia

Where is Doru? He was supposed to be home by now. I was talking to myself again. There is nothing interesting in the newspaper this morning. There never is. There is just the same old stuff about Ceausescu visiting different cities and something about politics. And there is always the page on local dissidents.

Hey, Mom! There's an article about two men that were retrieved from the Danube. It says they drowned probably while trying to cross the over into Serbia. The thought disturbed me.

Doru promised he'd be back by now! Could it be that he and Ludwig are the ones in the paper? He never even as much hinted that he might do something so crazy. What was he thinking? He has left me. And he left Liviu too! How am I going to pay the bills? Where are we going to get food? Why did he do this to us?

Convinced Doru and Ludwig were the drowning victims in the paper, I went straight to the police station to find out any available information. The policeman sat there as I told him the story of Doru and his friend Ludwig traveling to Bazias for the weekend. I told him I feared that they might have done something dreadfully wrong!

"Don't worry, lady. You'd have been notified long in advance had it been them," he coldly stated.

Somehow I was relieved to hear that and somewhat shocked at the policeman's air of certainty. But then I found myself backpedaling, trying to explain why I thought they might have tried to escape.

"Lady," he said. "It's more likely he just got mixed up with some other woman."

With that, I left—*mad*!

For several days, I stewed on what the policeman had said. That couldn't possibly be true. But Doru never mentioned, not even a peep, that he might flee to Serbia. What could I do but wait?

A week later, Doru was still missing. Worry, stress, and doubt overcame me. Could that policeman be right? Did he shack up with some boyhood girlfriend? My mother tried to persuade me that he likely escaped and that we would hear from him once he was free. It was incredulous to me. With little to do but wait, mother and I decided to get the mail. Lo and behold, there was a letter from Doru. Holy shit. It was stamped from Timişoara!

"You see! That policeman was right. Doru has run off with some whore! Why did he do that?" I asked my mother, telling her my plight. "He really has left us!" I was so mad.

"Wait a minute," mother interjected before I could rip up the envelope and cast it into the bin. "Open it up and see what it says."

"But I know what it is going to say!" I stormed knowing that I already hated the bitch! Mother gestured to me to open it. And so I did, grudgingly.

De, de, de, de . . . "Oh my god! Doru has escaped. It says he is in the refugee camp, along with Ludwig. They are in Trieste, Italy, and he will call me soon at work once he has the chance." I read aloud to mother. I was so happy. I was relieved but ashamed at what I had been thinking.

Shortly thereafter, I received an unwanted visitor. A man dressed in a black suit came to my work. He was from the *securitaté*.

"Rain Ofelia," he inquired.

"Ba da. Ce doriti?" Yes, I said, and asked what he wanted. He looked hard at me. His eyes stared down upon me as if accusing me of some wrongdoing.

"So your husband, Rain Doru, has left you," he said.

"Is that so?" I questioned him. I tried to hide my knowledge of Doru's whereabouts.

"Yes, it is. He has left you alone with your son. He has betrayed you. I could have you divorced in twenty-four hours because of his treachery, if you would like?" he said accusingly.

I told him that I loved Doru, and wherever he was, he would come back to me. But he pressed me several times more about divorce. He pressed to convince me that Doru had left me. He was not faithful to me. He remained faithful to Romania.

That really pissed me off. I continued to hide my anger at his line of accusation until he finally left.

* * * *

Toward the end of the first week, I received an appointment to meet for some further questioning. An officer came for me at the prescribed time and led me through a maze of corridors to a room toward the rear of the building. No one else was around. At the furthest point of a corridor stood a military officer guarding a closed door. As we approached, the guard opened the door and held it while I entered. A sophisticated-looking gentleman in a black suit greeted me. Immediately, the door was closed behind me. Maps were strewn upon a huge boardroom table.

He began, "Good afternoon, Rain Dragutin."

"Good afternoon to you too." I conjectured he must be from an intelligence agency. I imagined maybe Interpol or maybe even the CIA.

"We know who you are and where you are from. We even know where you worked. We know you have a wife, Ofelia, and a son, Liviu," He stated matter-of-factly. "I am here asking that you might help us clarify some details." The gentleman showed me a map, detailed beyond my imagination. It was of Reşiţa. He asked me to show him my apartment. There weren't any street names on the map, but once I orientated myself, I could clearly see my apartment. I had no idea that maps of this detail were even possible.

"Here is where I live," I said, pointing to the building.

"Does it look accurate?" he asked. I nodded my head in the affirmative.

He then produced another map, in an even smaller scale, of where I had worked. He pointed to my particular building and to my particular area in it. Amazed, and somewhat horrified, I asked myself where he could have gotten such information. More importantly, I wondered for what purpose they were questioning me. He pointed out several off ramps from the light-rail and asked if these were accurate. Pondering for a moment, trying to place them in my head, I recalled that these ramps were indeed there. But I had never seen a train there. I had heard that each industrial building had kept its own secret blueprints of how to make tanks. I had also heard that once given the orders, each factory could produce a tank a day. I imagined that was why the gentleman asked.

Upon my confirmation, he pulled out yet another map from below the others. This one was much different. I really couldn't believe it. I had practiced shooting a rifle here, as well as antitank weaponry. The field and the barracks were so well defined. There was even a dirt road on the map where tanks would practice maneuvers. I must have looked very bewildered at this point.

"It's OK. If you can qualify the accuracy, that is great. We are certain though that they are accurate," he stated.

It wasn't just the accuracy of the maps that astounded me; it was more of how they could possibly know that I had been there while in mandatory service. Had someone kept tabs on me? Not likely. If so, why? I was just a grunt soldier. He thanked me and led me back to the door. A guard was there to return me to my quarters.

Several weeks passed with little fanfare. Immigrants came, and some left. It was pretty boring. We were just waiting, for what, no one ever said. Then one late morning, Ludwig's relatives from Neutraubling, Germany, arrived in Trieste. Ludwig had gotten through to them, but they didn't know when they could come. They seemed a nice old couple. Ludwig and they embraced but not with the familiarity of someone very close. Ludwig introduced me. I think he was telling them I was the one whom he escaped with. We shook hands. And they continued to talk for hours in German. I didn't understand what they were saying. From time to time, they would look upon me. I started to feel self-conscious.

Finally, Ludwig came over to me to tell me that his relatives couldn't take me because I did not speak German. That seemed a poor excuse, I thought. At that point, I was shocked. That was part of the deal for helping Ludwig across the border. But in retrospect, I knew that Ludwig was a taker. He misled me from the start. He wouldn't have crossed the border to Yugoslavia without me. He wouldn't have even been able to swim across the Danube without my training. I spoke Serbian fluently and knew the boarder well. It was like the back of my hand.

With nothing to really say, I conceded, "Fine."

He gave me five hundred deutsche marks. In his own way, he was paying for my help. He gave me a hug and left.

Trieste : Doru, Lady and Ludwig

I felt abandoned and alone. Ofelia came to mind. She must have felt much the same, likely worse. Dejected, I had to raise my spirits somehow. With a new mission, I made my way downtown Trieste. There, after some questioning, I found the telephone company. There were several booths for international calling. Luckily, they weren't all being used. I dialed the number and waited for the connection from the operator. I hoped Ofelia was at work, somewhere near the telephone.

She answered. I was so happy. I told her of my adventure, where I was, and that Ludwig had left. She had already received my letter. She was happy to finally hear my voice. We talked about how she and Liviu were getting on. I had to apologize many times for leaving her behind. But I would get her away too once I got the chance.

Ofelia told me that she had already been visited by the *securitaté*. She said she had since talked to Viorel and Grandpa Jivko in Bazias. They had told Ofelia about Stefan's antics after Doru's disappearance.

* * * *

Stefan entered the community center just after 2:00 a.m. He came with a purpose. And that purpose was not to dance, drink, and enjoy himself. He approached one table with several military men. He asked them if they had seen Doru and his stranger friend. Of course, they had but didn't know where they were just then. He asked another table where Doru had been sitting earlier. Jivoine told him that we had just left. He told him that we were going to rest at my grandfather's. Stefan turned and then strutted quickly out. There was urgency in his step.

Once at Doru's grandfather's house, he knocked at the door. Grandfather went to the door.

"Where is Doru?" Stefan demanded. He had abandoned all decorum by not introducing himself. It was after 2:00 a.m. at this time. Grandfather affirmed that he was not there. He introduced the possibility that he and Ludwig had gone to his uncle's earlier. Stefan marched away, wasting little time. He did not find them there either.

Stefan then ran back to the base. He woke some of the men. They readied themselves to Stefan's orders. He was sure two men were attempting an escape.

They sounded the alarm.

Stefan readied himself. He leashed the dog and mounted a horse. He was on the chase. Several military men followed, including a soldier who now lives in Calgary.

First, they stopped at the guard shack. But the guard at the time had neither seen nor heard anything. It was quite breezy that evening. Stefan scolded him in a quick rant.

From there, the dog led them up the road toward Socol. Everyone proceeded at an urgent pace. There was no one there. There were no signs of Doru and Ludwig. The dog hadn't found anything either. A kilometer or two out of town, the troop stopped.

Stefan yelled, "If I catch Doru, I will kill him there and then!" They returned back to the village. The search was fruitless—for them.

* * * *

After Ludwig left, I started looking for work in Trieste. A lot of immigrants gathered at the train station. It was known by local Italians as a place to find cheap casual workers. Generally, they were looking for Serbian people or Serbian speakers.

I was there at the train station talking with some Serbians and other people when a black Maserati stopped. An Italian man was looking for two men to do concrete work for him. I never worked in concrete; but a Romanian Serbian guy, Florea Voina, from Romania told the Italian that he was an expert in concrete. The Italian man, Pepe was his name, hired both of us. We got into his car, and off we went.

He owned a retail clothing store. It was an old stone building, like the others that lined the street. Even the outside clearly needed some repair. He showed us into the basement storage room where repairs were sorely needed. The wooden floor had been built, likely when the building was constructed, directly onto the ground years ago. Over years of use, heat, and humidity, it had rotted and collapsed. What's even worse, mice scurried everywhere. It was a total gut job.

Pepe's brother took us to a building repair store. He kept saying "*sabia*." We were so confused. We interpreted it as the word in Romanian, which means "sword." Why does he need a sword? We kept saying to him "*calcio*." We needed calcium or cement to mix with sand. After some deliberations, and pointing to a pile of bags, we finally figured out that it meant "sand" in Italian. We bought the materials and tools we needed to lay a concrete floor. We were able to finish the floor in a couple of days.

Pepe was happy. He paid us and asked if we wanted to work in his clothing store. Because of its proximity to Yugoslavia, it was a popular place for Serbian-speaking clients. We accepted gratefully. He paid us ten thousand lire per day in cash. And if it was busy, he would even buy us lunch. Shortly afterward, maybe a week's time, my friend left for emigration.

I kept on with Pepe. The work was steady. I was able to save some money. He treated me well. So when I had the chance to introduce my new acquaintance, a Romanian named Zaharia Olaru, I did. Olaru did not speak Serbian and just a bit of Italian. He was in need for work. Pepe hired him on my recommendation. We worked for Pepe until we left for Latina. We shared a room at the camp; we ate together and became good friends. We bought a hot plate and cooked there in the room bacon, eggs, and sausages. We had to eat there in order to get to work on time. Breakfast in camp was a little later.

On the street where Pepe's store was, there were a few other businesses. There was a store called Zara run by a Serbian woman. We were talking once not long after I was informed that I would be going to Latina soon and then off to Canada. Concerned, she gave me a pair of winter boots and a winter hat. She feared I would be cold in Canada.

I really enjoyed my job. I met a lot of people and talked to a lot of Serbian customers. Some were quite regular. I became good acquaintances with one couple in particular. The man was actually from Bazias, and his wife was Romanian Serbian. From time to time, they were gracious enough to take a small package with gifts and money for Ofelia and Liviu.

In November, before Christmas, I purchased a nice yellow gold ring in Trieste for Ofelia. That evening after work, I stopped at the bar that was across the camp to have a beer and meet with people. I sat, as usual, at a table with Romanian people. One guy with a cast on his leg I knew well. Taqia was his name. He was from my hometown. We used to work together in Reşiţa. He was always lazy there and now, with his leg in a cast, enjoyed bumming cigarettes and a drink from everyone.

I showed them my ring. As they passed the ring from hand to hand, the conversation continued. After a little time, I asked, "Where is the ring?" to get it back.

"I don't know," said the first, then the second, and the third.

"Come on!" I retorted. No one said they had the ring. But Taqia's slightly gargled answer caught my attention. "Do you have my ring?" I asked.

"No," he mumbled again and shook his head.

I stepped up and smacked him straight in the jaw! And to my surprise, the ring popped out of his mouth and dropped onto the floor. "You son of a bitch!"

"You bastard! I should beat the shit out of you!" I yelled at him. But I didn't. "You lazy bastard! If you weren't already on crutches. You got what you deserve!" His mouth was bloodied from my punch.

The bartender, a big man, came from behind the bar. He saw everything and fortunately he knew me from my earlier times there. He picked up Taqia and several of the others and kicked them out.

Thank God, he didn't swallow it.

October 29: Work was uneventful today. We had stopped as usual at the bar, had a quick beer, and chatted with other immigrants on their way back to camp. From there, the walk back to the camp was quiet and pleasant.

Prior to dinner, everyone started to mull about, enjoying a cool late October evening. Then came a ruckus on our way to the room. Yelling, screaming, running. We stopped a couple people.

"There is a strange old man, with an ugly face. He ran at us and then disappeared," cried the couple. But we couldn't see anyone out of the ordinary.

The noise erupted again from another part of the camp. This time we ran toward it. There was nothing there again. But the same story persisted. An ugly faced man was there and now was gone. Kids were crying. "Jesuus Christ," why would someone frighten children? They pointed in the direction he escaped. And off we went.

As we approached others in that direction, they said they saw nothing. There was no strange, ugly-looking old man. No one scared them. Odd. No one seemed to be a reasonable suspect for creating the chaos.

A bit later, just before dinner, we heard another scream from behind the camp. We rushed over in that direction again. There we found Floria Sorin (a Romanian from Reşiţa). His face was covered in blood. He looked as though he had been in a fight. We guessed that maybe it was with the scary, ugly old man.

"Fuck!" Floria yelled. He had chased an ugly, scary man. "I got to within fifty meters of him. We were running like hell as I chased him behind the unlit portion of the building." Floria lost him right then. Floria had fallen off of the laundry deck down some three feet. He had screamed as he hit the ground. He was lucky to only break his nose.

We took Floria to the security office where we reported the incident. They called for the ambulance. Eventually, Floria was taken off to the hospital to be attended to. The incident and the ugly, scary man were the talk of the camp for quite some time.

However, it never happened again, and no one ever came forth with the name of the perpetrator. It remained a mystery . . .

A few months after getting there, we would all gather around and tell stories of how they escaped. One group had been there for some time longer than me. In fact, they were there for years. They had left during different circumstances in Romania, and no country was willing to allow them to immigrate. I felt sad for them and hoped I wouldn't become one of them. They told me they had escaped from Bazias. My interest peaked; I asked them how they escaped from there. However, even after so much time away from Romania, for some reason, they were not readily forthcoming. So I pressed them, "How did you get across from Bazias?"

"Ludwig and I swam across the Danube. You?" I asked them dubiously.

They looked at one another. Clearly they did not swim. Then they told me their story about a man from Bazias. They paid him many lei to get them across the Danube. Although they had not met him prior, many people knew of Saul. I knew him quite well. But I never imagined him in this illicit business. When I lived there, he was already an older man. His daughter had married the commander of the base in Bazias.

So hand in hand, Saul and the commander crafted a business of securing the transport across the Danube. The commander was sending guards the opposite direction to where the boat was scheduled to cross. Apparently, this had been going on for years under the nose of Stefan. I wondered if he too was involved.

The night that their group crossed, they remembered seeing a figure of a woman walking along the river. It was obvious to them that this woman had seen the whole affair. She had to know exactly what was going on.

As I pictured their escape, I was confused. Who could have been walking along the Danube in that area, at that time of night? Surely she would have been stopped as well by the military. Then I felt a lump in my throat. It came to me. Could it have been my mother? Sickened, it all made sense. She would not have been stopped or even questioned for being on the Danube. Everyone knew it was her job to check the level of the river.

So I pressed my suspicions and questioned them further. They said that Saul had since been questioned by authorities. They questioned his ability to have a new car and other extra things. Saul had been retired for some time. His pension would not have afforded his lifestyle.

Rumor has it that upon checking his house, one of the men accidentally stumbled and kicked a *damigeana*. The large glass wine decanter protruded from a corner. His boot broke the glass and out poured money. Lots of money!

The check of the house turned into a major investigation. Saul was arrested. He was charged. He eventually spilled the beans, and the police arrested the son-in-law commander as well. Both served several years in jail.

* * * *

I worked for Pepe until January 1980 when I was finally transferred to Latina.

Latina: Clouds Beginning to Clear

The train trip to Latina was uneventful. We had a short layover in Rome. There wasn't enough time to get out and explore. When I arrived at camp, they were very organized. They knew my name and all the details. Unlike Trieste, they were waiting for me. They assigned me a room. They informed me of mealtimes. And they told me not to bother them about any timing regarding my emigration. It was all controlled by the consulates.

It was evident that I could be here a while. So I just took my time. I slept and hung out for two weeks. Money really wasn't an issue as I had saved some while working for Pepe. When I finally got the energy to go exploring, it was more out of boredom.

Familiar from my time in Trieste, I asked a few people where workers would be found. The muster point was across the camp. On my first attempt, a Mercedes car stopped in front of me. A man pointed at me. He gestured to me to come closer. I complied. He asked if I was Romanian. Upon my confirmation, he told me to get into the car.

He introduced himself. His name was Euro Incerti. He was about fifty years old. He had a pizzeria and needed someone to work in the kitchen to do dishes and cut the veggies and cold-cuts for pizzas. He was paying ten thousand lire per day. Lunch and coffee were included. I accepted gratefully but told him that I had never worked in a kitchen. He said it's OK; he would teach me.

Euro turned out to be a very good man. I think he liked me very much as well. He introduced me to his family. At times, we also ate lunch together. We shared excellent conversations, as well as food and wine. They treated me very well. I worked hard for them.

One lunch, Euro asked, "Do you like my daughter?"

"Of course, I do. She is very lovely," I said. "Why do you ask?"

"Well, I think she likes you as well. If you were interested in staying in Italy, this could be the way," Euro replied. "You could marry her."

"Euro," I said. "You know I am already married. I have a loving wife and a beautiful boy. I really want to be with them once this ordeal is finished." He understood and never brought it up again.

Still, Euro and his family treated me we with respect. We remained friends.

On May 5, 1980, right after Tito of Yugoslavia died, I got on board a plane to Montreal, Canada.

Reşiţa: The Reign Slowly Loses its Grip

Ofelia

Doru's letter was safely in my pocket. I felt secure knowing it was nearby. That he was safe. The next day after receiving the letter from Doru, a *securitaté* officer showed up at my apartment door. I was caught a bit off guard. I knew someone would come; I just didn't think so soon. He had denim jeans and a gray button-up shirt more or less like everyone else. He wore normal street clothes. My apartment was still in disarray. We had just finished the floors, and I hadn't had time to rearrange the couch and the table. Surprisingly, he was rather pleasant—he had a kind, soft voice. He inquired if I was Rain Ofelia and several other questions to prove I was her.

He then questioned me, "Are you aware that your husband, Rain Doru, has left Romania?"

"Is that so?" I asked.

He interrogated me further. "He went to Bazias. Correct?"

"Yes, he did," I told him.

"That is when he escaped," he snapped. "Have you heard from him?"

"I got a letter from him. It came from Timişoara."

Incredulous, the officer asked more sternly in a commanding voice now. "You weren't aware that Doru was going to escape?"

"No, I wasn't aware! I love my husband. But he never ever mentioned leaving Romania," I responded.

It was true. Never once did Doru and I discuss anything like this. I wondered how long he had been having this idea. Did it start with Ludwig? Did he promise Doru something? As I thought back, not even Ludwig gave any hints or mention of their departure. Not even in jest. And they had just finished the hardwood floors. It was all so secretive. Yet I didn't feel like Doru had ever kept anything from me.

He asked to see the letter. I told him I had lost it in all the renovation mess. I did have the Timişoara stamp. Reluctantly, unconvinced, he left.

Doru continued to send care packages on a regular basis via a couple he had met in Trieste. The wife was Serbian and the husband Romanian. They had the fortunate situation whereby they could both leave and return from Romania. They had visa for both countries. Doru would put clothes, money, and, most importantly, food in it from Italy. And closer to Christmas, he surprised me with a beautiful gold ring. Doru may not have known, but the couple needed something from me as well. As part of this mutual arrangement, they needed me to sell some of their goods. This was the tricky part of the deal. All items from abroad were considered contraband. The *securitaté* was always on the lookout. I kept everything in very low profile. I knew the *securitaté* would try to trip me up, especially since Doru had escaped Romania.

I asked my cousin, Dolly, to help with selling some of the stuff. She worked at a textile company full of women laborers. They liked the clothes she had. Reluctantly, she agreed, and rightfully so. As we continued our little business, I had a suspicion that they were watching me very closely. I never saw anyone. I just had a bad feeling. And to my dismay, Dolly was caught in the act. The *securitaté* confiscated all the clothes, the tourist trinkets, and a set of pots. My mom had given the pots, with food, to me after she was done with work.

I felt so responsible for her predicament. I had caused it. I went to her father, a miner, and a very hardass to explain what had happened. He was pissed. However, he had a brawler's confidence that he could right the wrong.

In those days, miners had a special relationship with authority, in part, I think, because they had a sort of union that gave them a voice in government affairs. But also as likely, they were recognized as contributing to Romania with such hard and dirty work. To add, most of them were hardened and feared individuals. My uncle was no exception.

At the police station, my uncle began speaking to the officer in a soft, respectful manner. He explained that no harm had been done by such a young individual. She just had the misfortune of buying those goods for Christmas. She hadn't been selling them. The officer dismissed him at that point.

My uncle's character snuck out from the shadows. He told the indignant officer that he was starting to piss off a hardworking, well-connected miner. He then informed him that there was so much contraband clothing coming from Serbia. We have nothing here, and the trade has become part of Romanian livelihood. His fist struck the officer's bench. It shook like an earthquake. He then accused the officer of wearing a contraband shirt. Somewhat shaken. Indeed, he was.

My cousin joined as quickly thereafter. We swept her out of the police station.

In the middle of January 1980, Doru was transferred to Latina, Italy. Doru told me that he had no idea as to when he would be allowed to immigrate. In fact, he didn't even know to where he would be accepted. He had applied for Australia and Canada. Rumor was that the wait time for America was much greater. Immigration could take more than two years. Some of the people in Trieste had been there for several years. No countries wanted them. He prayed that would not be his final predicament.

In March, Doru was called to go to the Canadian Embassy in Rome. They told him that his application to immigrate to Canada had been accepted. They also felt that he would be sent there in relative short order. They asked if Doru had a family and if he wanted them to join him. The officer said they would be in contact with the Canadian Embassy in Romania. And that I would receive a letter from them in the near future. Shortly after his meeting, Doru called me at my clinic. He had good news. The Canadian Embassy had made arrangements for Doru to leave Italy for Canada on May 5, 1980.

I received a letter from the Canadian Embassy in Bucharest. Doru had already left Latina. He was safe in Canada. An application form was included in the envelope. I needed to fill it out and take it back to the Canadian Embassy in Bucharest. I needed it to be correct. Dr. Stoian was gracious enough to help me. But she only did so in the privacy of her office where there were no prying eyes. Another letter soon after was delivered to me. This one came from the city hall in Reşiţa, Internal Affairs Division. I was required to attend a committee meeting that oversaw my application for family reunification.

I felt uneasy that morning as I walked to the city hall. My throat was dry and scratchy, like I had eaten a quince. I didn't know what to expect. The thoughts of a committee meant I would be interviewed by more than one. How many would there be interrogating me—two, three, maybe four? It took me several minutes and some direction by others to find the room I was looking for. I described it more as a cinema. It was semicircular with cinema chairs. I estimated fifteen women sat in those chairs. In front of them, there was stage raised about two meters. On it, there was a long table. Eight intellectual-looking people sat behind it. I chose a seat by myself, a couple of chairs away from anyone else. My uneasiness turned more to anxiety. My heart pumped more rapidly and strong. I took a few deep breaths to relax. I was on the verge of a panic attack. Someone closed the entrance doors, and the interrogations began.

They called the first woman by name and directed her to come down from her seat to the front of the stage. She was the focal point of the committee and all her peers. They asked her some matter-of-fact questions. What was her legal name? What was her age? Where was she living? Was she married? Did she have children? She responded with trite unembellished answers. She was being interrogated as an accused at trial.

The committee continued with questions about why she wanted to emigrate from Romania. They asked why her husband had left Romania, why he left her, where was he going, etc. They seemed to be trying to embarrass her in front of us all. Perhaps she would change her mind. After maybe ten minutes of questioning, she was sent back to her seat. She had to stay to listen to the rest.

Another couple of women went through the exact questioning before my turn. At this point, a confidence came over me. I answered the questions without embellishing on anything. I offered no details unless directly asked. I too returned to my seat. I had no interest in listening to the other's plight.

Once everyone had been interviewed, the committee left the cinema. We followed a little behind. In the hallway, a woman approached me. She was one of the committee members. I wondered if my interrogation was not yet over. She asked me, "Where are you from, Ofelia?"

"Dognecea," I continued with curt answers. She appeared a little surprised.

"Who is your father?" she continued.

"Dumitru Alexa," I told her.

Her face gave a glint of sunshine. "I went to school with your father. We were only eight years old at the time." With that, she wished me luck and took her leave. That interrogation was done, but there would be many more each week.

That Thursday, and every Thursday from then on, a *securitaté* officer came to my work. I came to know him as Mr. Stanescu. He too, like the first one, was dressed in nondescript street clothes. He tried to convince me that Doru had abandoned me and only left Romania. He kept trying to find a crack in my armor. But I wouldn't let it break. He promised of a swift divorce. In twenty-four hours, it would be done. Doru's letters and his voice on the phone assured me. Maybe the spies were listening in? I loved Doru, and there was nothing anyone could do to destroy that.

I was fortunate to have such a good boss at the medical clinic. She understood my situation and allowed me time off when I needed. If it had been her boss though, I am not so sure. He was a true communist. He was as gruff as my uncle, but he held a high position as well.

Several months passed before I heard any news from the reunification committee. My application had been accepted. Right thereafter, I received more "official" mail regarding my emigration. One was a notice from the local authorities. They had frozen my rights to sell the apartment. Doru and I had worked so hard to pay sixty-six thousand lei. All that work for nothing. In fact, I was from thence forth required to pay rent. These legal papers stated that Romania had taken half of the value of the apartment from Doru and me. And to add insult to injury, the papers stated that by leaving Romania illegally, Doru had forfeited his remaining one-fourth share. Further to this, the state would pay me my one-fourth share. I couldn't even sell it myself.

I waited impatiently for my passport and visa to be returned to the Ministry of Foreign Affairs in Reșița. Every Thursday, I was required to go there to inquire as to my passport. The large room was always crowded. Many women would be there waiting to hear news as well. Their husbands had escaped as well. At the far side from the entrance, there were only two windows. One was for those traveling to Russia or another communist country. There were few people there. A man sat behind the glass, ready to do his job.

At the other window, for the traitors that were trying emigrate from Romania, a nasty old woman behind the glass controlled everything. We all waited our turn in line. We all wanted to know as to whether they had received our passports or had any news of its timing. She was a horrible old hag. I had to be as nice to her as I could. She wouldn't call you up unless she felt there was something for her. I brought B&V cigarettes for her just to acknowledge me. Once she took them, she'd say, in her raspy voice, "Nothing new." She didn't even have to look! Oh, she infuriated me.

At times, I suffered panic attacks at night. I would wake, seemingly startled, and sit right up. My heart pounded horribly. I had to take deep breaths to help it go away. I had to have Liviu sleep with me from then on. I would still have them, but the touch of his little hand calmed me more quickly.

Thursdays came and went with no news. Liviu was always with me. He hated going and wined his displeasure when we had to go. I could understand why, but I didn't always have my mother to look after him. It was always crowded in there. The perfume combined with the odor of cigarette smoke and sweat was always nasty. He was still short, and everyone bumped into him. And most times there were loud arguments among the women. They swore at one another.

As I turned away from the window, I recognized the backside of a man. Could it be? Why would he be here? The medical clinic boss turned, immediately recognizing me. He was somewhat startled. He knew why I was here. But I had no clue why he was here as well. Even such a strong communist member could lose his way. He asked me all kinds of questions about my experience in this affair. His wife had taken a trip to West Germany on a course. She refused to return. She sought political asylum. I empathized with him and offered as much as I could in advice. I am not sure what good it would be.

In August 1981, I met a long-lost acquaintance on the street. George Ciorobara, who had escaped before Doru and was living in New York, came back to see his mother. We were colleagues at the medical clinic. Ressi was her name. George had long, black hair. He wore gold necklaces and bracelets on his wrist. He was a contrast to what everyone else wore. As our conversation progressed, he asked if it would be OK to come over for a visit that evening. Without thinking much, I obliged. I invited my girlfriend and her boyfriend to meet him as well. They were to come around seven o'clock in the evening. So I waited outside and enjoyed the pleasant summer evening. George arrived in a big fancy car. Lots of people were outside then. We all checked out the vehicle.

Upstairs, I made some coffee. My neighbor, Elena Iovan, knocked on my door. I invited her in to meet my colleague's son from America. We were just having coffee and a smoke. She declined, said it was nothing, and left urgently. My dad came that evening as well. I had mentioned to him that George was in town. But by the time Dad arrived, everyone had left. Dad just wanted to meet George. He knew Ressi very well.

The next day, I went to work for my afternoon shift. My boss, Dr. Stoian, told me that I had to go to the police station. She told me that Mr. Stanescu, my regular Thursday *securitaté* visitor, needed to speak with me. She said I could go now before I started work.

At the police station, Mr. Stanescu showed me into what must have been an interrogation room. It was a small, rectangular room. There was a desk and two chairs—one in front and one behind it. He sat himself across from me and then asked me. I knew something different was taking place. I didn't have the normal feeling of him that I had grown accustomed to. He placed a paper and pen on the desk. "Who was in your apartment last night?" he interrogated me.

I was correct in my earlier assumption. I knew instantly that somebody had reported me to the police about George. My ears popped, and I started to see lights blinking in front of me. A panic attack was coming over me. I had known George for many years. Meanwhile, my head was hurting, thinking of who would be so malicious to inform against me. To me? I am sure he saw something on my face. He asked me what my boyfriend George and I were talking about when we were in the kitchen.

I told him the truth. I told him I knew who reported me too. They would call me in the middle of the night to give their kids injection when they are sick. He said not to mention names. I needed to use restraint and act accordingly with that person as before. I knew he sympathized with me and my stressful life.

Mr. Stanescu explained to me that only he and the chief of the police, Mr. Linta, were aware. He told me not to worry. He assured me that the incident would not affect my emigration papers. However, it was his duty to talk to me. This could be very serious though. He said that it was in the constitution. We were not allowed to have foreign citizens in our apartments. In fact, we were not allowed to talk to them on the street. George had become an American citizen.

The next Thursday at work, I opened to Mr. Stanescu. Somebody from the *securitaté* and a policeman in Dognecea paid a visit to my parent's house. The *securitaté* man was also dressed in plain clothes. At the time, my mom was alone. Dad was away working in Reşiţa. She was scared seeing the policeman at her door. She asked them what was wrong. Had they done something wrong? They said, "No, nothing happened. We just came to say hello and talk a bit." The *securitaté* man asked her if she had kids, and she told them. She told them that I lived in Reşiţa and worked at the blood bank. Further, he asked if I was married. She cried as she always did when it came to Doru. She loved him like a son until she died. She told him that Doru was in Canada and that I was waiting to leave Romania with Liviu. He became angry at that point. And he accused her of allowing us to leave with her grandson. Mother said yes. She added that Doru is such a good man. He loves my daughter and grandson.

And since I was on a role, I told him more. I had been on the bus and was lucky to get six eggs on my ration card. A well-dressed man approached me. He checked out my bag. The eggs were in it. He says to me that I was holding the eggs like you would American dollars.

Furthermore, another well-dressed man stopped beside me as I waited for the bus. I could see that his hands were soft and manicured. Without an introduction, he asked me my opinion on the ration cards.

I told Mr. Stanescu I knew those men were from *securitaté*. I felt like someone was always following me.

In January of 1982, I arranged for an appointment with the chief of the police, Mr. Linta. I told him that I had been waiting for more than two years to immigrate to Canada. I had become very impatient with the whole process. *What could possibly take this long*? I wondered. He called to the woman from the window in the lobby. She said there was nothing for me. The chief promised they would notify me upon its arrival. That is not what I expected to hear. I was supposed to get my passport; I didn't even know.

The weeks continued to pass. I became ever more intolerant. My panic attacks were more frequent and at times more debilitating. I knew that every Thursday that passed meant I had less time on my visa to get ready to emigrate. The police chief's promise turned out to be hollow. In a mood of sorts, with another pack of Kent in hand, I pushed passed the stinky Thursday crowd toward my window. I heard my name. An elderly man called my name again from the other window. He signaled with his finger to approach him. To my surprise, the regular nasty old woman wasn't behind the other window.

"Doamna Rain," he said. "We have your passports and visa here." He told me that it had been there for some weeks. *That hag!* I screamed to myself. He noticed that our visas to leave the country were about to expire. I only had a couple of weeks. I was shocked and dismayed. He gave me the passports and told me to go to Bucharest immediately. I needed to see the minister of external affairs. There, I should tell them that our passports just arrived. We needed to extend the visa so that I could put my affairs in order. In the meanwhile, he suggested that my husband should buy plane tickets for me and my son. If we needed to go through America, we would also need a transit visa from the American Embassy in Bucharest. He warned me that I would need money to pay for a stamp, a kind of tax, in order for them to process my request. But they could and should be able to do it right away. He was a kind, sympathetic old man.

I was so grateful I wanted to hug him.

On the way out, I heard several women gossiping. Apparently, the old hag had been beaten up by someone who felt mistreated by her.

With urgency now at hand, I needed to expedite my trip to Bucharest. My boss continued to be gracious at my absence request. And with what, I told her about the big boss man. She gained more confidence. Fortunately, our emigration extension request was granted as per the old man. That would be the only easy event in my travails. I told Doru to get plane tickets, and sure enough, we were going to New York.

The next day, March 15, 1982, back in Reşiţa, I informed Dr. Stoian that I was quitting. She helped me in one hour to have my resignation papers checkmarked. At home, another letter awaited me. I was informed that I should evacuate the apartment almost immediately. We were being evicted. In the notice, they included a form. I needed to get the proper paper work of the resignation of my work. I needed to get to all the utilities to ensure all bills were paid. Each box on the form needed to be filled out and stamped before I would be allowed to leave Romania.

Getting the money from the state before my evictions was another matter. I received a letter informing me of a scheduled meeting to get my funds. I had to go the internal ministry. The ministry was housed in one of the taller buildings in Reşiţa. The department I needed to visit was on the seventh floor. To make things worse, the elevator was out of service. I climbed those stairs, letter in hand. I thought this was not fair that we had worked so much to come to so little. The only fortunate part of the whole affair was that another girl from my medical clinic had been selected to occupy the apartment.

I entered the room. There were a few people doing business and several workers behind the counter. I was able to get the attention of one of them. She asked me my name and required my letter as well as credentials. She went away, to some back room, leaving me standing at the counter. I waited impatiently. She returned, looked up at me, and said simply that they didn't have the funds ready. I held back my frustration for a moment. She offered nothing else. Then I lost it on her. Her reply, come back in a week. She didn't care. She wasn't even sure they would have the money then. This was so frustrating.

Dr. Stoian called me at home and said that Madame Wide Load had my money ready. I should go immediately to city hall to get it. The elevator was still not working. There was the big woman behind her desk. I closed the door behind me and turned to address her. She threw the money at me. All over the desk and on the floor were one hundred lei bills. What had she done? I picked up the money. I glared at her and said sharply to her, "Did you keep any of the money for you?" The other workers looked at us flabbergasted. "Well, if you didn't, you are not getting any from me." I counted every last bill. I walked out.

I paid my final bill for electricity and gas. Both were the highest I had seen the whole year. I just paid.

At the city hall, they told me that I had to bring them my apartment keys. Another nurse was going to move in. I found out her name. I knew who she was. I asked her to let me stay until April 5. I had to leave Reşiţa the next day. She said not to worry.

A few days before the fifth, I went to the city hall for the last time. The last thing I had to do to satisfy the authorities was to give back my apartment keys. I knew the man there. I had earlier done blood tests for his kids to attend day care. I didn't require a blood donation.

Now he asked me for the second key. I said that I had only one. He didn't believe me. I was lying.

"I won't stamp and sign the paper until you bring me the second key," he countered.

I got upset. I asked him why he was treating me like a stranger. I reminded him that I helped him and his wife. "Besides," I said, "what would I do with the key? I am leaving Romania!"

He made up some stupid excuse about my family was maybe going to be staying there.

Indignant now, I told him not to worry. I wrote my father's address on a scrap of paper. If somebody from my family will be there, they can go and arrest him. He accepted my explanation and stamped and signed my paper.

The apartment was empty. I sold as much as I could. The rest I gave to my family. My dad, my mom, Liviu, and I sat on the floor. There was only an ashtray and a bottle of vodka. I cried with Mom and Dad. I knew that this was it. I may never see them again. My parents accompanied Liviu and me on the train to Bucharest the next day. We rented a nice suite in a hotel in Bucharest. We talked all night. In the morning, we shared a taxi to the airport. I gave my dad all the money that was left over from sale of the apartment. We said goodbye.

1982—Getting Out of the Reign

Ofelia

Where were we going? All I could think about was the address and phone number that I wrote on Liviu's ankle. Prior to leaving for the airport, the *securitaté* warned me not to bring any documents. Any documents referencing my marriage, my birth date, or even the address of where I was going would be discarded in a prejudicial manner. So I left everything behind except for the hidden writing on Liviu's ankle. I couldn't remember Doru's phone number. It had a strange seven digits to it compared to our six.

It struck me as odd how many Romanians were on our flight to New York. They all must be in the similar sort of circumstances as us. Nobody talked about it though. I was frightened. Even now, aboard this plane to New York, there could someone spying on us. They would send us back. I had our passports tight to my bosom so as not to lose them. The nearer we got to New York, the more frequently I reached for them. I had to ensure that they were still there. Liviu pretty much sat there, saying nothing, looking out the window, seeing nothing but ocean. He was as comfortable as could be.

Several hours into the flight, I knew we were nearing New York. I couldn't understand any of the flight attendants. They all spoke English. There was a beehive of activity not long after an announcement on the speakers. We joined into the commotion as well. I asked Liviu to put his shoes back on. But first, I needed to remember the numbers I had inscribed on the inside of his shoe. Anxiety, panic, and madness struck me simultaneously as I scolded Liviu. His face looked at me with concern. He did not understand what had gone wrong. The writing on his shoe was partially gone! He had sweated and his socks had rubbed away much of the address. What were we to do now? I thought to myself, trying desperately not to panic.

The stewardess came around and put our tables up and our seat backs forward. She said something to us. I did not understand at all but nodded my understanding. I should have studied my English better was all I could think. Anyway, Liviu and I sat there waiting for the plane to land, and sure enough, it soon did.

LaGuardia airport was an ominous place. It was filled with all sorts, especially black people who worked there in the baggage. Strange and foreign as it all seemed, Liviu and I made our way through customs. We got our baggage. Then I was lost!

I found a person who looked to have some authority. I showed him our ticket—Air Canada. He pointed to the door where we found ourselves on the street curb. It was so cold! There was so much snow. We struggled to get our bags outside.

I knew I had to transfer planes. The trick was trying to find someone who didn't speak Romanian but who would understand what I needed. And then I needed him to be kind enough to direct us. With great trepidation, I approached one of the black porters. I showed him our remaining travel vouchers. I shrugged, hoping he would get the idea of my quest.

My fears were allayed as he called us a cab. Maybe fifty meters away, the black cabbie asked me something. I shrugged in return. He stopped immediately, got out, and emptied our luggage from the trunk. We quickly found ourselves back on the curb. He understood that we had no money to pay for the ride. Liviu and I walked the rest. And we made it none too soon. We were ushered directly aboard the flight.

Several hours later, we landed in Calgary. I prayed Doru would be waiting there for us. I couldn't take the stress of another New York moment. Everything was foreign here as well. The signs meant nothing to me. I gripped Liviu's hand firmly and followed the rest of the passengers as they made their way. The crowd formed lines. I later realized we were at customs. With my free hand, I reached toward my bosom for the relief of knowing that our passports were still with me.

I handed our passports reluctantly to the woman behind the counter when it was our turn. She looked at the documents; then she looked back at us. I thought I heard her say something for which I gave no answer, so I shrugged instead. The second time she asked something, I put my free hand to my mouth, motioning to her that I could not speak English. She nodded her understanding and then made a motion, pointing to the ring on her finger. That struck some sort of cord with me, and I showed her mine too and smiled. I figured, but still am not sure, if she asked who was waiting for us. With that ceremony accomplished, Liviu and I set off again. We found the luggage area. It was obvious we had to collect our bags, but still without the familiar faces from our plane, I would not have known where to go.

Again, with my hand firmly gripping Liviu's, but now with our luggage, we followed the others out of the luggage room into the portico of the airport. Lots of people gazed at and around us. Where was Doru? I couldn't see him. I told Liviu to keep a look. Then off with a shot, he pulled away from my hand.

"*Tati, tati!*" Liviu shouted. He ran to a man with long hair and a big handlebar moustache. I could not believe my eyes. Three years without his daddy, and he had no doubt who that strange-looking man waiting for us was.

1989—The Reign Stops

In the winter of 1989, we heard about a struggle for change in Romania. It seemed so far away from the safety of Calgary, but it really peaked our interest that maybe something important was about to happen there. The media of the event was really quite scarce as I am sure the *securitaté* was keeping all foreign journalists away from the event. We had heard through friends that the military had shot at a crowd of protestors in Timişoara and killed many.

In December, very near Christmastime, we saw on TV the mass crowd in Bucharest. However, instead of seeing a crowd cheering in a support rally, we were astonished to hear boos and the shouting of "down with Ceausescu." I remember his face and its utter disbelief.

Thereafter, we were shocked watching the video and the photos of his capture, summary trial, and execution of both Nicolae and his wife, Elena.

Ofelia

When I saw Ceausescu get out of the personnel carrier, there were strange feelings in my heart. He wore a hat that reminded me of my father as an old man, helpless, a victim of his own circumstances. I actually cried, knowing that his fate was sealed. And yet, I felt jubilation mixed with fear of the changes that were ahead. Thankfully, we were in Canada. But the pain he caused left its mark on me for many years. I would go shopping almost every day just to ensure the food was still available in the stores.

* * * *

Back in Romania, I heard similar feelings among the population. The elders were frightened of what lay ahead. The youngsters were out in crowds celebrating their freedom, which was previously only a notion heard on the radio via Free Europe. The *securitaté* stayed in their homes. Otherwise, they would be recognized by the crowds in the streets as the perpetrators of the crimes. Neighbors strangely enough left them alone, as they recognized them as fathers. My dad had the opportunity to confront Elena. We all knew what she did. My dad and mom were visiting Resiţa when they saw Elena on the street. As always before, she came over to them. She tried to hug them. But this time, they deflected her. She asked about me, Liviu, and Doru. My dad then shamed her. Finally, he accused her of her past transgressions. How could you get so low and inform the *securitaté* about my daughter? Did they pay you? She did not say a word in her defense. She just put her head down and fled down the road.

The military manned the streets. They kept a semblance of order. The masses recognized them as comrades. They had disobeyed and betrayed Ceausescu's orders to fire their machine guns into the crowds. I am certain Romania would have been much different had they not betrayed him.

In an expression of their newfound freedom, the population partook in all things earlier forbidden to them. First, they openly discussed the wrongdoings of Ceausescu. Second, they freed all the political prisoners who suffered terribly at the hands of the *securitaté*. Finally, they traveled to visit friends and family in foreign countries.

Everyone had different experiences that they will remember for the rest of their lives. It was a very important time. Delia, our friend now in Canada, told us that for her eighteenth birthday, she went to Hungary. While in Budapest, she ate ripened bananas and drank a Coca-Cola for the first time. Christina, another friend in Canada, remembered trying to do her part to help those that suffered during the fighting that ensued. She went down to the blood bank to make a donation. In her weak and malnourished state, she became very weak, and the nurses felt they could not continue. However, Christina insisted and lay back on the bed so as not to faint. She made her donation. She left only once she felt stable to go home.

Until this time, the thought of returning to Romania, even to visit what remained of my family, had never crossed my mind. I was glad to be in Canada, proud to be a Canadian, and thankful that Ofelia, Liviu, and my youngest brother, Viorel, were here by my side. Family back home in Romania apparently had different ideas.

1982: There were many Romanians living in Calgary at that time. Richmond Road had some sort of attraction. Coincidentally, some of them actually came from the same immigration camp in Trieste. On several evenings, we gathered at a popular restaurant. We talked about our journeys. We told stories of our travails. Everyone at that camp remembered the arrival of the Asians. They also reminisced about the night of the ugly, scary old man. One man, Floria, sat there smiling wryly. He sat quietly, minding his business.

I asked him, "What do you think?" That is when he confessed to being the strange, scary old man. Remember, it was Halloween! Many of us had never ever heard of it until coming to Canada.

1989: This year, my buddy who owned the car with the sticker, immigrated to Canada. Winnipeg was their first new home. He had brought his wife and two daughters. We visited them several times before they eventually moved to Vancouver. I lost touch with them.

1999: Twenty years after my escape, I received a call from one of the new TV series *Surprize Surprize* in Romania. They had been airing a show where those who had left Romania years before, and had never returned, were given the opportunity, on the request of remaining family members, to come back and visit their homeland.

My family had won!

In December, before St Nicolas, Viorel and I traveled back to Romania for the first time in many years. I was excited to be part of *Surprize, Surprize.* I was curious to see how my family was doing. I was skeptical that anything had changed since the removal of Ceausescu.

Everything at the airport was arranged for us. A driver picked us up there and checked us in to a good hotel. It was the one where the communist party used to meet. How fitting. We were met there by a beautiful woman, the star of the show, Marin Andrea. She explained what would happen on the show and told us to enjoy ourselves.

At the studio, Viorel was given a disguise. He put on a dark vest and a taxi driver's hat. One of the makeup people stuck a big mustache on his lip. We waited behind the stage for our turn to act. I hadn't seen the show on TV before since it was never broadcast in Canada. I really didn't know what to expect. From behind the curtains, we could see Marin Andrea on the stage with a woman. She was interviewing her regarding her request to bring an old boyfriend back to Romania. They had shared a very intense and loving affair many years ago. I didn't hear the whole story correctly, but somehow they found themselves separated. He abruptly left Romania, leaving her behind. She loved him still to this day. To the audience`s and our surprise, a man on a white horse road onto the stage. The crowd clapped. He stopped near Andrea and the lady. The man dismounted the horse, got onto one knee, held out his hand, and proposed to her! It was all so magical.

The crowd clapped and cheered. It was a heartfelt affair. The host, Andrea, stepped down from the stage. She walked into the crowd, over to where my brother, Nicolae, and his son were sitting. They had come to watch the show at the behest of Andrea. She had called them and said their application had won the free trip to see the show. She interviewed them both now.

"Rain Nicolae, when was the last time you have seen your brother?" she asked. The cameras pointed at them.

Nicolae responded, "It has been twenty plus years since he escaped."

"Well, we have arranged for him to come to Romania." I could see Nicolae's face change. "However, we have heard that he has been delayed at the airport." A phone rings. It was someone from the studio, saying that they are on the way with a taxi.

That was Viorel's cue. He started the jeep and drove it up onto the stage just like the horse had. I got out. Andrea turned back to Nicolae. "I guess he has arrived!" The crowd clapped and yelled as Nicolae made his way up to hug me. He was so surprised. We both were crying. Andrea let us have a moment.

Then she asked, "So your older brother, Doru, is here. When was the last time you saw your younger brother, Viorel?"

Viorel was already out of the jeep, next to us. He tore off his hat and the big bushy mustache. Nicolae looked at him in amazement. Clearly, he didn't recognize him in disguise!

What a great way to be welcomed back to Romania.

2011: Thirty years after my escape, my son, Liviu, traced my journey from Romania, through Yugoslavia, and into Italy. A lot had changed by then. He couldn't find Pepe, and Euro had since died. Liviu did meet his daughter, who remembered me. She told Liviu that I was a good, friendly, and respectful man.

2015: Liviu was wed in 2015 to Nicole Elizabeth Basden. Their wedding was held in Vancouver. Many of his friends from Calgary and Vancouver were present. He even invited my lost buddy's family, who Liviu stayed in touch with. However, my buddy wasn't there. I inquired with the family. However, neither his ex-wife nor his children had seen him for some time. That afternoon, I can only explain it by the grace of God, he walked past the church. I recognized him across the road. I ran over to him and tapped him on the shoulder. He turned. He did not recognize me. I began to talk to him in Serbian. He smiled as he remembered me as his long-lost pal from Socol grade school. The whole family came over. It was an emotional remembrance. Everyone cried.

TRANSCRIPT OF THE CLOSED TRIAL OF NICOLAE AND ELENA CEAUSESCU

Military base Tirgoviste—December 25, 1989

*** PROSECUTOR Gica POPA ***

General Gica POPA, "killed himself" in March 1990?

A voice: A glass of water!

NICOLAE CEAUSESCU: I only recognize the Grand National Assembly. I will only speak in front of it.

PROSECUTOR: In the same way he refused to hold a dialogue with the people, now he also refuses to speak with us. He always claimed to act and speak on behalf of the people, to be a beloved son of the people, but he only tyrannized the people all the time. You are faced with charges that you held really sumptuous celebrations on all holidays at your house. The details are known. These two defendants procured the most luxurious foodstuffs and clothes from abroad. They were even worse than the king, the former king of Romania. The people only received 200 grams per day, against an identity card. These two defendants have robbed the people, and not even today do they want to talk. They are cowards. We have data concerning both of them. I ask the chairman of the prosecutor's office to read the bill of indictment.

CHIEF PROSECUTOR: Esteemed chairman of the court, today we have to pass a verdict on the defendants Nicolae Ceausescu and Elena Ceausescu who have committed the following offenses: Crimes against the people. They carried out acts that are incompatible with human dignity and social thinking; they acted in a despotic and criminal way; they destroyed the people whose leaders they claimed to be. Because of the crimes they committed against the people, I plead, on behalf of the victims of these two tyrants, for the death sentence for the two defendants. The bill of indictment contains the following points:

Genocide, in accordance with Article 356 of the penal code. Two: Armed attack on the people and the state power, in accordance with Article 163 of the penal code. The destruction of buildings and state institutions, undermining of the national economy, in accordance with Articles 165 and 145 of the penal code. They obstructed the normal process of the economy.

PROSECUTOR: Did you hear the charges? Have you understood them?

CEAUSESCU: I do not answer, I will only answer questions before the Grand National Assembly. I do not recognize this court. The charges are incorrect, and I will not answer a single question here.

PROSECUTOR: Note: He does not recognize the points mentioned in the bill of indictment.

CEAUSESCU: I will not sign anything.

PROSECUTOR: This situation is known. The catastrophic situation of the country is known all over the world. Every honest citizen who worked hard here until 22 December knows that we do not have medicines, that you two have killed children and other people in this way, that there is nothing to eat, no heating, no electricity.

Elena and Nicolae reject this. Another question to Ceausescu: Who ordered the bloodbath in Timisoara. Ceausescu refused to answer.

PROSECUTOR: Who gave the order to shoot in Bucharest, for instance?

CEAUSESCU: I do not answer.

PROSECUTOR: Who ordered shooting into the crowd? Tell us!

At that moment Elena says to Nicolae: Forget about them. You see, there is no use in talking to these people.

PROSECUTOR: Do you not know anything about the order to shoot?

Nicolae reacts with astonishment.

There is still shooting going on, the prosecutor says. Fanatics, whom you are paying. They are shooting at children; they are shooting arbitrarily into the apartments. Who are these fanatics? Are they the people, or are you paying them?

CEAUSESCU: I will not answer. I will not answer any question. Not a single shot was fired in Palace Square. Not a single shot. No one was shot.

PROSECUTOR: By now, there have been 34 casualties.

Elena says: Look, and that they are calling genocide.

PROSECUTOR: In all district capitals, which you grandly called municipalities, there is shooting going on. The people were slaves. The entire intelligentsia of the country ran away. No one wanted to do anything for you anymore.

UNIDENTIFIED SPEAKER: Mr. President, I would like to know something: The accused should tell us who the mercenaries are. Who pays them? And who brought them into the country?

PROSECUTOR: Yes. Accused, answer.

CEAUSESCU: I will not say anything more. I will only speak at the Grand National Assembly.

Elena keeps whispering to him. As a result, the prosecutor says: Elena has always been talkative, but otherwise she does not know much. I have observed that she is not even able to read correctly, but she calls herself an university graduate. Elena answers: The intellectuals of this country should hear you, you and your colleagues.

The prosecutor cites all academic titles she had always claimed to have.

ELENA CEAUSESCU: The intelligentsia of the country will hear what you are accusing us of.

PROSECUTOR: Nicolae Ceausescu should tell us why he does not answer our questions. What prevents him from doing so?

CEAUSESCU: I will answer any question, but only at the Grand National Assembly, before the representatives of the working class. Tell the people that I will answer all their questions. All the world should know what is going on here. I only recognize the working class and the Grand National Assembly -- no one else.

The prosecutor says: The world already knows what has happened here.

I will not answer you putschists, Ceausescu says.

PROSECUTOR: The Grand National Assembly has been dissolved.

CEAUSESCU: This is not possible at all. No one can dissolve the National Assembly.

PROSECUTOR: We now have another leading organ. The National Salvation Front is now our supreme body.

CEAUSESCU: No one recognizes that. That is why the people are fighting all over the country. This gang will be destroyed. They organized the putsch.

PROSECUTOR: The people are fighting against you, not against the new forum.

CEAUSESCU: No, the people are fighting for freedom and against the new forum. I do not recognize the court.

PROSECUTOR: Why do you think that people are fighting today? What do you think?

Ceausescu answers: As I said before, the people are fighting for their freedom and against this putsch, against this usurpation. Ceausescu claims that the putsch was organized from abroad.

CEAUSESCU: I do not recognize this court. I will not answer any more. I am now talking to you as simple citizens, and I hope that you will tell the truth. I hope that you do not also work for the foreigners and for the destruction of Romania.

The prosecutor asks the counsel for the defense to ask Ceausescu whether he knows that he is no longer president of the country, that Elena Ceausescu has also lost all her official state functions and that the government has been dissolved.

The prosecutor wants to find out on which basis the trial can be continued. It must be cleared up whether Ceausescu wants to, should, must or can answer at all. At the moment the situation is rather uncertain.

Now the counsel for the defense, who was appointed by the court, asks whether Nicolae and Elena Ceausescu know the aforementioned facts—that he is no longer president, that she has lost all official functions. He answers: I am the president of Romania, and I am the commander in chief of the Romanian army. No one can deprive me of these functions.

PROSECUTOR: But not of our army, you are not the commander in chief of our army.

CEAUSESCU: I do not recognize you. I am talking to you as simple citizens at the least, as simple citizens, and I tell you: I am the president of Romania.

PROSECUTOR: What are you really?

CEAUSESCU: I repeat: I am the president of Romania and the commander in chief of the Romanian army. I am the president of the people. I will not speak with you provocateurs anymore, and I will not speak with the organizers of the putsch and with the mercenaries. I have nothing to do with them.

PROSECUTOR: Yes, but you are paying the mercenaries.

No, no, he says. And Elena says: It is incredible what they are inventing, incredible.

PROSECUTOR: Please, make a note: Ceausescu does not recognize the new legal structures of power of the country. He still considers himself to be the country's president and the commander in chief of the army.

Why did you ruin the country so much: Why did you export everything? Why did you make the peasants starve? The produce which the peasants grew was exported, and the peasants came from the most remote provinces to Bucharest and to the other cities in order to buy bread. They cultivated the soil in line with your orders and had nothing to eat. Why did you starve the people?

CEAUSESCU: I will not answer this question. As a simple citizen, I tell you the following: For the first time I guaranteed that every peasant received 200 kilograms of wheat per person, not per family, and that he is entitled to more. It is a lie that I made the people starve. A lie, a lie in my face. This shows how little patriotism there is, how many treasonable offenses were committed.

PROSECUTOR: You claim to have taken measures so that every peasant is entitled to 200 kilograms of wheat. Why do the peasants then buy their bread in Bucharest?

The prosecutor quotes Ceausescu, Ceausescu's program.

PROSECUTOR: We have wonderful programs. Paper is patient. However, why are your programs not implemented? You have destroyed the Romanian villages and the Romanian soil. What do you say as a citizen?

CEAUSESCU: As a citizen, as a simple citizen, I tell you the following: At no point was there such an upswing, so much construction, so much consolidation in the Romanian provinces. I guaranteed that every village has its schools, hospitals and doctors. I have done everything to create a decent and rich life for the people in the country, like in no other country in the world.

PROSECUTOR: We have always spoken of equality. We are all equal. Everybody should be paid according to his performance. Now we finally saw your villa on television, the golden plates from which you ate, the foodstuffs that you had imported, the luxurious celebrations, pictures from your luxurious celebrations.

ELENA CEAUSESCU: Incredible. We live in a normal apartment, just like every other citizen. We have ensured an apartment for every citizen through corresponding laws.

PROSECUTOR: You had palaces.

CEAUSESCU: No, we had no palaces. The palaces belong to the people.

The prosecutor agrees, but stresses that they lived in them while the people suffered.

PROSECUTOR: Children cannot even buy plain candy, and you are living in the palaces of the people.

CEAUSESCU: Is it possible that we are facing such charges?

PROSECUTOR: Let us now talk about the accounts in Switzerland, Mr. Ceausescu. What about the accounts?

ELENA CEAUSESCU: Accounts in Switzerland? Furnish proof!

CEAUSESCU: We had no account in Switzerland. Nobody has opened an account. This shows again how false the charges are. What defamation, what provocations! This was a coup d'etat.

PROSECUTOR: Well, Mr. Defendant, if you had no accounts in Switzerland, will you sign a statement confirming that the money that may be in Switzerland should be transferred to the Romanian state, the State Bank.

CEAUSESCU: We will discuss this before the Grand National Assembly. I will not say anything here. This is a vulgar provocation.

PROSECUTOR: Will you sign the statement now or not?

CEAUSESCU: No, no. I have no statement to make, and I will not sign one.

PROSECUTOR: Note the following: The defendant refuses to sign this statement. The defendant has not recognized us. He also refuses to recognize the new forum.

CEAUSESCU: I do not recognize this new forum.

PROSECUTOR: So you know the new forum. You have information about it.

Elena and Nicolae Ceasescu state: Well, you told us about it. You told us about it here.

CEAUSESCU: Nobody can change the state structures. This is not possible. Usurpers have been punished severely during the past centuries in Romania's history. Nobody has the right to abolish the Grand National Assembly.

The prosecutor turns to Elena: You have always been wiser and more ready to talk, a scientist. You were the most important aide, the number two in the cabinet, in the government.

PROSECUTOR: Did you know about the genocide in Timisoara?

ELENA CEAUSESCU: What genocide? By the way, I will not answer any more questions.

PROSECUTOR: Did you know about the genocide or did you, as a chemist, only deal with polymers? You, as a scientist, did you know about it?

Here Nicolae Ceausescu steps in and defends her.

CEAUSESCU: Her scientific papers were published abroad!

PROSECUTOR: And who wrote the papers for you, Elena?

ELENA CEAUSESCU: Such impudence! I am a member and the chairwoman of the Academy of Sciences. You cannot talk to me in such a way!

PROSECUTOR: That is to say, as a deputy prime minister you did not know about the genocide? PROSECUTOR: This is how you worked with the people and exercised your functions! But who gave the order to shoot? Answer this question!

ELENA CEAUSESCU: I will not answer. I told you right at the beginning that I will not answer a single question.

CEAUSESCU: You as officers should know that the government cannot give the order to shoot. But those who shot at the young people were the security men, the terrorists.

ELENA CEAUSESCU: The terrorists are from Securitaté.

PROSECUTOR: The terrorists are from Securitaté?

ELENA CEAUSESCU: Yes.

PROSECUTOR: And who heads Securitaté? Another question . . . .

ELENA CEAUSESCU: No, I have not given an answer. This was only information for you as citizens.

CEAUSESCU: I want to tell you as citizens that in Bucharest . . . .

PROSECUTOR: We are finished with you. You need not say anything else. The next question is: How did Gen. Milea {Vasile Milea, Ceausescu's defense minister} die? Was he shot? And by whom?

ELENA CEAUSESCU: Ask the doctors and the people, but not me!

CEAUSESCU: I will ask you a counterquestion. Why do you not put the question like this: Why did Gen. Milea commit suicide?

PROSECUTOR: What induced him to commit suicide? You called him a traitor. This was the reason for his suicide.

CEAUSESCU: The traitor Milea committed suicide.

PROSECUTOR: Why did you not bring him to trial and have him sentenced?

CEAUSESCU: His criminal acts were only discovered after he had committed suicide.

PROSECUTOR: What were his criminal acts?

CEAUSESCU: He did not urge his unit to do their patriotic duty. Ceausescu explains in detail that he only learned from his officers that Gen. Milea had committed suicide. The prosecutor interrupts him.

PROSECUTOR: You have always been more talkative than your colleague. However, she has always been at your side and apparently provided you with the necessary information. However, we should talk here openly and sincerely, as befits intellectuals. For, after all, both of you are members of the Academy of Sciences.

Now tell us, please, what money was used to pay for your publications abroad -- the selected works of Nicolae Ceausescu and the scientific works of the so-called Academician Elena Ceausescu.

Elena says: So-called, so-called. Now they have even taken away all our titles.

PROSECUTOR: Once again, back to Gen. Milea. You said that he had not obeyed your orders. What orders?

CEAUSESCU: I will only answer to the Grand National Assembly. There I will say in which way he betrayed his fatherland.

PROSECUTOR: Please, ask Nicolae and Elena Ceausescu whether they have ever had a mental illness.

CEAUSESCU: What? What should he ask us?

PROSECUTOR: Whether you have ever had a mental illness.

CEAUSESCU: What an obscene provocation.

PROSECUTOR: This would serve your defense. If you had had a mental illness and admitted this, you would not be responsible for your acts.

ELENA CEAUSESCU: How can one tell us something like this? How can one say something like this?

CEAUSESCU: I do not recognize this court.

PROSECUTOR: You have never been able to hold a dialogue with the people. You were not used to talking to the people. You held monologues and the people had to applaud, like in the rituals of tribal people. And today you are acting in the same megalomaniac way. Now we are making a last attempt. Do you want to sign this statement?

CEAUSESCU: No, we will not sign. And I also do not recognize the counsel for the defense.

PROSECUTOR: Please, make a note: Nicolae Ceausescu refuses to cooperate with the court-appointed counsel for the defense.

ELENA CEAUSESCU: We will not sign any statement. We will speak only at the National Assembly, because we have worked hard for the people all our lives. We have sacrificed all our lives to the people. And we will not betray our people here.

The court notes that the investigations have been concluded. Then follows the reading of the indictment.

PROSECUTOR: Mr. Chairman, we find the two accused guilty of having committed criminal actions according to the following articles of the penal code: Articles 162, 163, 165 and 357. Because of this indictment, I call for the death sentence and the impounding of the entire property of the two accused.

The counsel for the defense now takes the floor and instructs the Ceausescus once again that they have the right to defense and that they should accept this right.

COUNSEL FOR THE DEFENSE: Even though he—like her—committed insane acts, we want to defend them. We want a legal trial. Only a president who is still confirmed in his position can demand to speak at the Grand National Assembly. If he no longer has a certain function, he cannot demand anything at all. Then he is treated like a normal citizen. Since the old government has been dissolved and Ceausescu has lost his functions, he no longer has the right to be treated as the president. Please make a note that here it has been stated that all legal regulations have been observed, that this is a legal trial. Therefore, it is a mistake for the two accused to refuse to cooperate with us. This is a legal trial, and I honor them by defending them.

At the beginning, Ceausescu claimed that it is a provocation to be asked whether he was sick. He refused to undergo a psychiatric examination. However, there is a difference between real sickness that must be treated and mental insanity which leads to corresponding actions, but which is denied by the person in question. You have acted in a very irresponsible manner; you led the country to the verge of ruin and you will be convicted on the basis of the points contained in the bill of indictment. You are guilty of these offenses even if you do not want to admit it. Despite this, I ask the court to make a decision which we will be able to justify later as well. We must not allow the slightest impression of illegality to emerge. Elena and Nicolae Ceausescu should be punished in a really legal trial.

The two defendants should also know that they are entitled to a counsel for defense, even if they reject this. It should be stated once and for all that this military court is absolutely legal and that the former positions of the two Ceausescus are no longer valid.

However, they will be indicted, and a sentence will be passed on the basis of the new legal system. They are not only accused of offenses committed during the past few days, but of offenses committed during the past 25 years. We have sufficient data on this period. I ask the court, as the plaintiff, to take note that proof has been furnished for all these points, that the two have committed the offenses mentioned. Finally, I would like to refer once more to the genocide, the numerous killings carried out during the past few days. Elena and Nicolae Ceausescu must be held fully responsible for this. I now ask the court to pass a verdict on the basis of the law, because everybody must receive due punishment for the offenses he has committed.

The final speech of the prosecutor follows:

PROSECUTOR: It is very difficult for us to act, to pass a verdict on people who even now do not want to admit to the criminal offenses that they have committed during 25 years and admit to the genocide, not only in Timisoara and Bucharest, but primarily also to the criminal offenses committed during the past 25 years. This demonstrates their lack of understanding. They not only deprived the people of heating, electricity, and foodstuffs, they also tyrannized the soul of the Romanian people. They not only killed children, young people and adults in Timisoara and Bucharest; they allowed Securitaté members to wear military uniforms to create the impression among the people that the army is against them. They wanted to separate the people from the army. They used to fetch people from orphans' homes or from abroad whom they trained in special institutions to become murderers of their own people. You were so impertinent as to cut off oxygen lines in hospitals and to shoot people in their hospital beds. The Securitaté had hidden food reserves on which Bucharest could have survived for months, the whole of Bucharest.

Whom are they talking about, Elena asks.

PROSECUTOR: So far, they have always claimed that we have built this country, we have paid our debts, but with this they bled the country to death and have hoarded enough money to ensure their escape. You need not admit your mistakes, mister. In 1947, we assumed power, but under completely different circumstances. In 1947, King Michael showed more dignity than you. And you might perhaps have achieved the understanding of the Romanian people if you had now admitted your guilt. You should have stayed in Iran where you had flown to.

In response, the two laugh, and she says: We do not stay abroad. This is our home.

PROSECUTOR: Esteemed Mr. Chairman, I have been one of those who, as a lawyer, would have liked to oppose the death sentence, because it is inhuman. But we are not talking about people. I would not call for the death sentence, but it would be incomprehensible for the Romanian people to have to go on suffering this great misery and not to have it ended by sentencing the two Ceausescus to death. The crimes against the people grew year by year. They were only busy enslaving the people and building up an apparatus of power. They were not really interested in the people.

Post Haste

Ten and Two

Calgary AMA—Driving Instructor:

My student kept his hands in the prescribed position, as we made our way east down Seventeenth Avenue in Calgary. He was a very conscientious young man and asked me often what I thought of his progress. He was doing quite well, I thought, and told him so. As we neared the apartment complexes, he pointed up at one of them and said, "My sister used to live there."

"Really?" I remarked. "Did she move away recently?"

He hesitated. His hands were back at ten and two on the steering wheel. Oddly, he asked, "Do you really think I am becoming a good driver?"

"Yeah, I think you are making good progress, and soon, with more practice, you will make a good driver."

A small smile came to his face. "That's good to know because my sister died in a car accident not long ago, and I don't ever want my poor driving to be the cause of an accident."

Daryl's first novel recounts the real-life story of Doru Rain. As Doru and his friend Ludwig try to elude capture from the *securitaté*, the tragedy of Doru's family reveals the hardships of life under the reign of dictator Nicolae Ceausescu. Along the way, his father dies, his mother drowns, and the necessities of life disappear. Doru, desperate for a better life, risks all as he flees the country, even leaving his young family behind.

Daryl Robbins was born in St. Catharines, Ontario. He spent his youth playing competitive hockey, golf, and track and field before accepting a scholarship to Princeton University. There, he was a member of the Cap & Gown Club and earned a degree in geological and geophysical sciences. After graduating in 1990, Daryl pursued a career in oil and gas exploration in international projects. In 1997, he returned to Canada. Currently, he lives in Calgary, Alberta, where he continues his career as a partner in a project management company. Here, he met Doru and Ofclia Rain, the subject of this real-story book—Escape the Rain.

Resita : The Rain Family

Vancouver : Rain Family

For my wife Ofelia, my son Liviu and his wife Nicole, and my grandchildren Lucas and soon to be born baby, my brothers Nicolae and Viorel, and all my friends and relatives.

Thank you Daryl.

God Bless you all.
Doru